BUDO TRAINING
IN
AIKIDO

BUDO TRAINING IN AIKIDO
Written by Moritaka (Morihei) Ueshiba, founder of Aikido

Translated into English by Larry E. Bieri (© in Japan)
　　　　　　　　　　　　Seiko Mabuchi (© in Japan)

All rights reserved
Copyright © 1997 by Kisshomaru Ueshiba

Published by Sugawara Martial Arts Institute Inc.
20-13, Tadao 3 Chome, Machida-Shi, Tokyo, 194 Japan
ISBN: 087040-982-4

First printing: July 1997
Printed in Japan

Distributors;
United States: Kodansha America, Inc. through Oxford University Press, 198 Madison Avenue, New York, NY 10016
Canada: Fitzhenry & Whiteside Ltd., 195 Allstate Parkway, Markham, Ontario L3R 4T8.
United Kingdom and Europe: Premier Book Marketing Ltd., 1 Gower Street, London WC1E 6HA.
Australia and New Zealand: Bookwise International, 54 Crittenden Road, Findon, South Australia 5023.
The Far East and Japan: Japan Publications Trading Co., Ltd. 1-2-1, Sarugaku-cho, Chiyoda-ku, Tokyo 101, Japan.

BUDO TRAINING
IN
AIKIDO

Sugawara Martial Arts Institute / Japan Publications

UPON REPUBLICATION OF ENGLISH EDITION

This book, written by founder of *Aikido*, Morihei Ueshiba, was published as a revised English edition adapted to the current new age. I am very grateful for this significant publication.

Throughout his life Morihei Ueshiba wrote only two books on *Aikido*. This *"Budo Renshu"* (original name) was the first of two. I remember how he had been devoted to its work while it was still in preparation.

Recently, the spirit of Aikido has gained world wide recognition which is the reason for which I believe it can serve greatly in the role as a new guiding principle in the education of today's youth which must bear the next generation.

At the beginning of the *Showa* era (from 1926 onward), *Aikido* had not been popular when compared with other competitive martial arts seen in tournament, since in *Aikido* the mind and the body was trained internally without the use of competition. Recent *Aikido* has received recognition from other martial arts fields which made me remember many situation of those past days, filling me with deep emotion.

I hope that many people will read this new book with appreciation and use it as mental nutrition in every day training. If this should occur, then this revised edition will have great significance - not only Mr. Tetsutaka Sugawara, who put in quite an effort in the publication of this book, but also many other people share this wish including the founder now in heaven, Morihei Ueshiba, who is greatful for this publication.

I sincerely want proper *Aikido* to be trained.

TRANSLATOR'S INTRODUCTION

We would like to begin by thanking Doshu Ueshiba Kisshomaru and the Aikikai Foundation for making this family treasure available for publication. We also wish to express our appreciation to those teachers who gave their invaluable help in explaining difficult passages.

Due to the historical nature of this work certain difficulties arose, especially in deciding to what degree we should try to produce clear and precise English. Any precise translation could easily become a personal translation, limiting the contents and range of the translator's individual understanding at this particular point in his or her training. Therefore, after consulting some of the highest Sensei in Aikido and other arts it was decided to strive for a translation that would both preserve the simplicity of the original expression and at the same time leave open to the reader at least the possibility of coming up with the broad set of ideas and associations indicated in the Japanese.

This book appeared in 1933 and is the first published account of O-Sensei's art. Although not actually written down by him, it is a transcription of lectures and explanations which was later reviewed by the founder and approved as a teacher's manual. The political and historical context of the times should be kept in mind. No attempt has been made to edit the text.

The original copy has O-Sensei's title which was simply "Budo Renshu", i.e. "Budo Training". Later the second Doshu annotated this with the word "Aikido". The Dojo decided on using the original name here despite the fact that most Japanese copies are entitled "Aikijujutsu Ogi", or "The Secrets of Aikijujutsu". The latter is actually an interpretive heading used by the copyists.

The original was hand-written and illustrated. Later this was copied out several times, using tracing paper to reproduce the illustrations. During this process errors easily crept in. By comparing various copies, most of the poems could be deciphered despite their flowerly writing style. However only a few of the tracing mistakes have been corrected here. In other cases the terms 'left' and 'right' had been reversed. This seems to be the result of confusing Nage's point of view with Uke's. In this edition these obvious errors have been corrected to match the illustrations.

The poems presented the biggest problems. Much effort was spent to offer the reader a translation which presents as closely as possible the same degree of lee-way for interpretation, insight and error, as appears in the original. Two versions are offered. One reflects the 5-7-5-7-7 syllabic structure of five line, Japanese Waka poetry. Each line in English contains the same groups of words found in the corresponding line of Japanese. The second attempt is to put the poem into a somewhat clearer English syntax. Another interesting point about the poems is that not all of them are original compositions of O-Sensei. At least a few can be traced to other martial traditions.

Please note that the parentheses indicate the insertion, for your reference, of a Japanese word used in the text for the preceding English word (except for a few cases in the technique section where O-Sensei used parentheses in the original). Square brackets are the translator's insertions for the sake of the English. By simply deleting the sections enclosed by them, they allow readers to refer to O-Sensei's exact words, if they choose to do so.

Although not for the beginner, it is hoped that access to this historically important text will be useful in understanding Aikido and its origins for those who have taken Budo as their 'Way'.

Larry E. Bieri
Seiko Mabuchi

Contents

UPON REPUBLICATION OF ENGLISH EDITION.......(5)

TRANSLATOR'S INTRODUCTION.......(7)

PREFACE.......(11)

The Secret Teaching of Budo (Poems).......(13)

The Essence of Technique.......(21)

    STANDING TECHNIQUES.......(22)

        1. Shomen.......(22)

        2. Yokomen.......(23)

        3. Kata [Shoulder].......(23)

        4. Munamoto-Dori.......(25)

        5. Tekubi-o-tsukamu-koto (Grabbing Wrists).......(25)

    USHIRO-WAZA (Rear Techniques).......(27)

        USHIRO-ERI (Back of the Collar).......(28)

Technical Illustrations and Explanations.......(29)

    SUWARI-WAZA (Sitting Techniques).......1

        Shomen (Front or Face on).......1

        Yokomen (Side of the Head [strike]).......3

        Kata (Shoulder).......4

        Sode (Sleeve).......5

        Ryosode (Both Sleeves).......7

        Mune (Chest).......8

        Kubijime (Choke or Strangle Hold).......11

        Te (Hand).......16

Hanmi-Handachi (Half Sitting Half Standing).......24

TACHI-WAZA (Standing Techniques).......41

Shomen (Front of Face on).......41

Yokomen (Side of the Head [strike]).......50

Kata (Shoulder [grabbed]).......60

Sode (Sleeve).......78

Kata (Shoulders).......100

Te (Hands), Katate (One Hand).......106

Aikinage.......108

Kokyu, (Ryote (Both Hands)).......121

Shiho Nage.......122

Mune (Chest; Collar, Neck).......137

Mune to Te (Chest and Hand).......150

Kubijime (Strangle Hold).......154

Ushiro-Eri (Back of the Collar).......168

Kata (Shoulder).......177

Ude (Arms).......188

Tekubi (Wrist).......194

PREFACE

Bu derives from God's own substance and mind, and is a major spiritual component of the truth, goodness and beauty embodied in the founding of our nation. *Bujutsu* arose along the way of the Imperial nation and lays its foundation on the sincerity of *Kotodama*[1] expression coming from the *Aiki*[2] between Man and the hundreds of gods (*Kami*)[3]. Moreover this sincere mind, which we call the *Yamato Spirit*, is attained through training the body. By trying to unite the body in this spirit, which is oneness resulting from the training of the sincere soul, Bujutsu takes as its purpose the building of the sincere man, possessing the spiritual oneness and unity which allows not the slightest opening between the body and the spirit.

As soon as Man is born, he encounters troublesome times. However, if you train in such as way that every encounter is seen as a major crisis, that is, as true *Shugyo*[4] or as a vitally important trial, then you can go back and forth between the arenas of the living and the dead and it becomes possible to transcend the very idea of life and death. The main thing is to attain the "Way" which opens up [reality] calmly and clearly, just as in "every-day" situations, no matter what kind of terrible crisis or dangerous events you may face.

In olden times it was said the *Bu* was conveyed from the gods to the Emperor, and then to the military commanders. There is wisdom in this; namely, that this "Way" realizes the genuineness of the Imperial way. With this in mind, we understand and embody the truth of Heaven and Earth and, for the sake of governing the universe, master worldly affairs inside our stomachs by means of the Universal *Kokyu*[5] and our own breathing. We come to express the sincerity of genuine spiritual unity and oneness-of-soul which takes charge of the masses with its technique of oneness and instructs us in the way of governing the nation, of pacifying the public, of dispersing evil and of spreading the right law. The main purpose [of *Bu*, then,] is to enhance the prestige of the Empire and to bring light to the whole nation.

[The contents of] this book were taught taking in consideration the time, place and the mentality of the participants at the summer school of *Showa* 8 [1933].

As social conditions change and the human mind progresses, [your] *Bujutsu* should continually shift direction, under the guidance of [your] senior. But, by reading this book and training, understanding of the true meaning of *Bujutsu* will grow unconsciously and you will become a true master.

Moreover, since this book will be passed down to the trainee who has received its instruction as a sort of certificate of achievement, the author sincerely asks the trainees to build up [a store of] hard training experience every day under [qualified] instruction [in order to] master the essential techniques and to proceed onto more advanced ones.

The Secret Teaching of Budo
(Poems)

1. **'Bu received from the gods at the beginning of the world,**
   Is ours for protecting the nation';
   The Emperor's exhalted voice!

   At the beginning of the world
   Calm down
   The purpose of "Bu" in
   The protection of the nation;
   The Emperor's exalted voice [proclaims]

2. **At the dawn of time descended**
   Magatama*, mirror and sword,
   Symbols of gods' will to found a nation

   At the dawn of time
   Descended
   Magatama, mirror and sword
   A nation to build (through)
   The will of the gods

   NOTE: * *Magatama*: the 'comma-shaped' stone or jewel used as a symbol of royalty on the continent and in Japan, (during the late stone age and bronze age).

3. **Give in to the Universal Breath of the gods**
   Become a warrior who builds
   The Will of the *Kami*

   The multiplicity of our gods!
   To the breath of the Universe
   Give in to
   The will of the gods,
   As a warrior, I build

4. **Come to appreciate the perfect balance of "*Izu* and *Mizu*"*:**
   'The Cross of *Aiki*'**
   Then, through the voice of the positive, advance courageously

   The precious
   "*Izu* and *Mizu*" in
   The "*Aiki-Ju*"
   Courageously advance
   in the voice of "*Izu*"

   NOTE: * *Izu* and *Mizu*: the Yang and Yin aspects of the individual soul or spirit, that together make up one's spiritual side. *Izu* is active (Yang, Japanese "*Yo*"), and *Mizu* passive (Yin, Japanese "*In*"). Note that *Mizu* is a homonym of the word for water while *Izu* carries a feeling of to 'gush out' or spring forth'.

   ** The cross of *Aiki*: literally "*Aiki-Ju*", a cross or X-shape with 2 arms of equal length intersecting perpendicularly at their centers, i.e. +. One arm represents the positive aspect and the other negative side. In the case of labeling the arms "*Izu* and *Mizu*", the resulting balanced shape symbolizes the 2 aspects of the individual soul in harmony with and within itself.

5. **Self-delusion leads one down an evil trail**
   Do not give rein to your spiritual horse.

   Self-delusion or doubt
   To an evil way
   Will lead
   To the spiritual horse
   give no rein.

6. ***Jo-Dan* must be empty of self,**
   Then in that way
   One can cut down the thrusts of spears and win.

   As for *Jo-Dan*
   A selfless *Jo-Dan*

In this way
The attacks of spears
Can be cut down, and you can win.

7. Should your enemy take *Ge-Dan*
   Stay as you are in *Chu-Dan*;
      Do not move your weapon up or down

The enemy [takes] *Ge-Dan*
[Stay] In the same *Kamae*,
In *Chu-Dan*
Neither raise nor lower
Change not [your stance]

8. Progress only comes with constant practice
   Built up and kept to oneself
Do not hope for 'secret teachings'
   They will lead you nowhere

Progress?
Both practice and the [resulting, inner] experiences
   Must be stored up
Do not hope for secret teachings
There is no future in that

9. Spearheads to the front
   Thrusting shafts to the rear,
      The enemy everywhere!
But with the spears as your shield
   Cut your way to victory

To the front and to the rear
Spearheads and butts
The enemy!
With the spears as your shield
Cut [your way] in and win

10. Chop off and throw away the delusions
   Of cutting or parrying, of left or of right

Use the spirit to rush in instantly

Left and right
Cutting and blocking
Discard them all
[Rather] with the spirit of entering
Go in instantly

11. Without the slightest *Suki**, discard all thought
   Of the enemy and his encircling ring of swords,
      Just jump in and cut!

With no *Suki*,
Attacking and encircling
Swords of the enemy
Discarding it all
Step in and cut.

NOTE: * *Suki*: an opening; an unguarded place, vulnerable to attack.

12. Should an enemy come running and strike,
   Avoid him with a step to the side
      Then attack in an instant.

One of the enemy
Comes running
When he strikes
Take a step to avoid [him]
And cut instantly

13. One who is always prepared for any event
   Need not use his blade rashly or in haste.

Any person [who]
No matter what happens
Is well prepared
In haste, his sword

Must never use.

**14. If to weaken the enemy is to your intent,
First step inside and cut**

If the enemy's sword
to weaken
Is your plan
First step in and close
Then cut

**15. Though surrounded by a crowd of the foe,
Fight with the thought that they are but one.**

A multitude of enemy
Encircles me
Though they attack
As a single foe
I view them
As I fight

**16. In the midst of a forest of enemy spears,
Know their very tips as your shield**

Surrounded!
Into a forest of spears
I have entered
As a shield the spears'
Tips you must know

**17. Each time before the gods I stand,
That blessed Way of *Izu* and *Mizu*
Floods my mind**

Again and Again
Each time I go to worship
I recall
Izu and *Mizu*
That blessed Way

**18. A forest of opposing swords is led
With the enemy's spirit as your only shield**

Standing in opposition
A forest of swords
Is led
As a shield, the enemy's
Spirit, I take

**19. To realize the Ultimate Truth of the Unity of the Two Worlds,
Ceaselessly cultivate sincerity with all your heart**

Sincerity
More and more with all your heart
Practice and perfect
The essential Unity of the Two Worlds
Come to know its truth

**20. *Bujutsu* is the form and spirit of the goods,
Precious parent(s) of *Izu* and *Mizu***

Bujutsu is
The form of the gods
And their spirit
Izu and *Mizu*'s
Precious parent(s)

**21. Call out the perverted enemy
Advance and set him straight by the sword of the gods
All for the sake of the Way**

For the sake of the Way
The perverted enemy
Call out, and set him straight
Proceed in the word
And the sword of the gods

22. Thinking I am in front of him

**The enemy raises his sword to attack
But lo, I am already standing behind him**

Raising his sword and
Thinking I am before him
He flies in to attack
But to the enemy's rear
I am already standing

**23. Drawing out the attack of the perverse enemy,
My body stands behind him and cuts**

The warped enemy
Is caused to attack
My form
Behind him standing
Cuts the enemy down

**24. When challenged by a single enemy
Watch out!
You are always surrounded**

When challenged
Even by a single foe
Watch out!
A herd of enemy
Surrounds all sides

**25. Once you divinely master the techniques of *Aiki*,
No enemy would ever think of attacking**

If by the gods
The *Aiki* techniques
You have mastered
No form of enemy
Would ever attack

**26. Pour your soul into daily practice
To take charge of events in the spirit of oneness
Is the 'Way of the Warrior'***

Day by day for technique
Pour your heart into training
Through oneness
Command the miriad things
The Way of the Warrior

NOTE: * The Way of the Warrior: "*Monoonfu no Michi*", literally 'the Way of the Warrior or Fighting Man'. The more familiar term "*Bushi*" as in "*Bushido*" actually is a term of class or caste, indicating the hereditary position as a member of a warrior family, or the way of the *Bushi* caste in the feudal social structure.

**27. Embody 'Yang' in your right hand
Turn the left into 'Yin'
Then guide your foe**

With the right hand
Embody the 'Yang'
The left hand
You change into 'Yin'
Now lead your foe

**28. Why hopelessly fix your eyes on the sword he is swinging
His grip will tell you where he is cutting**

The swinging sword
To catch with the eye,
Will lead to naught
His grip
Is where he is cutting

**29. What use to learn this sword work or that!
Cut off all thought of useless things**

This and that
Sword work you may learn
But for what?
Just completely
Cut off thought [of useless things]

30. With the 'Sword of Initiative' held in the Heavens
    Close in quickly
Swing it around and
    Cut [down] diagonally

With the "*Sen no Tachi*"
Positioned in the Heavens
Close [in] quickly and
Swinging it around
Cut diagonally

31. Standing in the mountain stream I wonder
    Why it is no one can speak
As purely as
    The water sounds against the stone

In the mountain stream
I stand
But like the sound of the torrent
Speaking clear and true
I find no man

32. Enlightenment
    Like the hazy moon of evening
        Comes out and sets without a trace

Enlightenment!
[Was it] that man?
Like the evening moon
Rising and setting
No one knows at all

33. Master the voice that shouts "Yah!"
    See through to reality
        Remain unmoved by the enemy's ploys

To see reality
The voice of "Yah!"
Must be mastered
The enemy's rhythm
Must not affect you

34. With *Jo-Dan* you must judge
    The enemy's state of mind
        So view his Yin spirit as Yang

In *Jo-Dan*
The enemy's spirit
You must judge
Take the mind of "*In*"
And see it as "*Yo*"

35. With the foe's mind at the center
    You assume *Chu-Dan*
Then take care of his movement
    With a flick of the wrists

In *Chu-Dan*
The foe's mind
Into the center
[You watch] his rhythm
With the same grip

36. In your *Ge-Dan*
    You must see
        His Yang mind as if Yin
And know the jabs of his sword
    To be but *Seigan*

In *Ge-Dan*
The mind of "*Yo*"
Must be seen as "*In*"
And the thrusting blade

Known as *Seigan*

37. Realizing in your heart
   That life and death looms before you
      You might wish to withdraw
   But the enemy will not let you

Life and death
Stand before our eyes
Know this well!
Though we would retreat
The enemy will not allow it

38. When you instruct
   Emphasize the strike and thrust
   For all the secret teachings
      Are to be found in simple basics

In teaching,
The rhythm of strike and thrust
Listen well to,
Training in secret teachings
Is in the "*Omote*"*[basics]

NOTE: * *Omote*: Here refers to the first level or *Kihon* of training i.e. the basics. In many classical traditions the term is used as the name of the first set of Kata. Modern Aikido uses it to indicate movements which are performed in "front" of the *Aite*, as contrasted with "*Ura*" techniques where one stands generally "*behind*" him.

1 **Kotodama**: literally "Speak-Spirit". Translated as the "soul or power of language", it is associated with the intrinsic power of certain sounds and other esoteric practices.

2 **Aiki**: as often in Japanese this term "meet" (*ai*) carries the idea of reaching an accord between two sides. Here it may imply a thorough, mutual understanding.

3 **Kami**: a diety, an exalted spirit, but usually not the omnipotent God. This term is both singular and plural. Furthermore, the component sounds of *Ka* and *Mi* are associated in *Kotodama* theory with the characters *Ka* or "fire": and *Mi* of "water" (More commonly read *Mizu*). These two characters are in turn two of the five Chinese-Japanese cosmological elements, the others being, according to most theorists, *Ki* or "wood", *Do* or "earth", *Kin* or "metal". Each element was associated with the dualistic nature of the universe as expressed by the theory of *Yin and Yang* (Japanese, I*n-Yo*). Fire is *Yo* (*Yang*) and water is *In* (*Yin*). Thus, the term *Kami* is seen as an expression of the unity of *In* and *Yo* and is used to imply such nuances throughout this essay, as well as with its normal nuances. Conversely the terms "fire and water" can be read as a reference to the idea of *Kami*.

4 **Shugyo**: training, practice, ascetic practices, discipline, pursuit of knowledge.

5 **Kokyu**: breath, respiration; knack, secret.

The Essence of Technique

STANDING TECHNIQUES

1. Shomen

This term means striking with the right or left hand [to your *Aite*'s[1] face].

Since in any technique to strike the enemy with the *Tegatana* [or the fist] the breathing of the Universe and Man's own breathing must be the same, the attack should be made calling into the *Tegatana* both movement and the technique of unifying Yin and Yang.

If you face an enemy who is coming to attack in this manner and always block with a broad or imposing frame of mind as if enveloping the enemy inside your *Kokoro* (mind, heart or spirit), you will be able to tell the enemy's movement in advance. Then, attuning yourself to this [premonition] you can turn your body to the right or the left accordingly. Or if you embrace the enemy into your mind or spirit (*Kokoro*), you will be able to lead him in whatever direction the universe might indicate [to you].

For example, by showing the enemy an opening in your defense where he should strike, you can make him attack accordingly and overcome him by evading to the right or left. You can stand above the border between life and death and command a view of every situation so that even if you have received 99% of the enemy's pressure and entered into the realm of death you will still be able to seek out the way [to go], clearly.

You must train with these things in mind.

In the old days, when training in military strategy was held on a limited area of *Tatami*, it was comparable to training the *Kokyu* which fights by grasping the spirit of the whole of Heaven and Earth, according to the way. In this case, you have taken the proper distance (*Kyori*)[2]. In *Kendo*[3], this is the principle of *Suigetsu*[4] ("water and moon" or solar plexis); that is to say, using the distance or spacing as if it were a position of water, (such that [your weapons] do not yet cross). In other words, you face placing a physical and spiritual distance between yourselves. When the enemy attacks with fire you defend with water. When you invite your enemy to strike, water should surround you from start to finish and you should move within that water. The same thing is said of old castles. Only when there is a moat can you call it a [true] fort. Around the castle there is water to prevent an attack from the enemy. As for the human body, when the enemy comes to strike you, open up [as] with water so that you cannot really be struck. In the case of a [well-built] castle, if the people who defend it do not have fidelity (*Makoto*), it will fall, regardless. But in Japanese strategy, *Budo* training means actual people transferring this form of castle into their human bodies and building, therein, a living fortress.

Everything in the world works in this way. If you look at Japan, being surrounded by the sea, it forms a natural castle so that an army of devils cannot attack it very easily or recklessly. To defend this [our nation], each person must build a castle inside himself and then consolidate all these castles together. This is the training of *Budo*.

If you look at the whole world, we see that it cannot be crushed because it is composed of water. Moreover on a larger scale it is enclosed by icebergs. The earth itself has its magnificent defenses, and likewise the universe has its own. Each person who practices *Budo* helps defend the great castle of Mother Nature which is governed by the gods and should be training to build an even more beautiful one.

With this state in mind, both striking or being struck should be accomplished by means of *Kokyu* (breathing or breath) that is in line with this truth. When this is mastered, wisdom, benevolence and courage spring naturally from within you and make the one, true *Yamatodamashii* (Japanese spirit); you are able to make your whole body become as a sword and you can enter into a spiritual state of 'Selflessness' (*Muga-no-kyochi*). All Budo can build a beautiful nation of the spirit inside your body as you go from [one level of] *Satori* to another.

Speaking on a larger scale, we defend the whole nation and on a small scale we defend our own body. Ultimately it is the exercising and perfecting of *Yamatodamashii*. It is the same as the ceremonial "Opening of the Great Stone Door" (*Iwato-biraki-no-gyo*)[5]. Moreover, if the human mind once takes charge of water and fire, in accord with the principle of "Water-Fire, Yin-Yang", when your enemy attacks with water, you strike with water, with fire then hit with fire. Today, it is important to train thinking (all this) in terms of modern scientific (chemical) warfare.

2. Yokomen

This term means striking the enemy's *Yokomen* (side of the head) or cutting him diagonally downward from the joining of the neck and the shoulder with the *Tegatana* (hand blade).

When seeing the enemy's movement invite in his *Ki*[6] and step back slightly with your left foot dissipating his impetus (*Ki*). Then, without losing this chance and with the intention (*Ki*) of attacking him with "Yin-Yang (water-fire)", grab and pull his right (left) wrist to your left front. Bring your right hand onto it, [as well], then take a big step in with your left foot and while turning to the right throw him to your right front with the breath of "Yin-Yang". This technique can be applied in a wartime situation where the enemy's vanguard and yours clash and their main force moves to your left side and attacks your front and left side. You can cut down diagonally from your front to you left, just as with a sword, and at the same time advance with your crack unit [best effort] toward the enemy who is threatening your right side, and then, by attacking their main force, destroy the force that threatens your right side. Under such strategy, this *Yokomen* movement is played out everyday on the mat. In other words, it is the strategy applied at the moment you and your enemy meet and used during the march. The strategy which skillfully utilizes topographical conditions and materials. So we have our strategy [in *Jujutsu*] divided into *Jo-Dan*, *Chu-Dan* and *Ge-Dan* and *Ku-Den*, but these should be handed down during training, [so we will leave them for now].

[Speaking of] *Ken-po*[7] (if we were to dwell on small points), [we may mention that] when the enemy goes up to *Hasso*[8] stepping back with his right so as to cut down, if you think well on the idea of the Principle of *Suigetsu*, you can cut in straight to his front so that he is unable to use his sword. Moreover, in *Ken-po*, we also learn to pull back to the left in *Hasso*, that is to say, the way to cut down to the left; we study the *Ken-po* where we cut to the right while stepping in with the left foot; and also cutting the enemy who is behind us by turning our body. The techniques of *Yokomen-Uchi* were put together to learn these four *Ken-po*.

3. Kata [Shoulder]

Grabbing the shoulder of a relaxing, off-duty soldier is easy, whereas trying to grab him after the fight has started is most difficult. That is when you [must] blind the enemy as you grab his shoulder with your left or right hand.

When the enemy grabs hold of your shoulder, you should parry his attempt to blind you with your left hand, or when he pulls after he has gotten hold of your shoulder, you should take advantage of his movement to strike his *Men* with your right hand and to punch his solar plexis with your left hand; then throw him down to his right rear corner.

In this *Bujutsu*, you should be especially careful to completely unify your mind, body and strength. Strength is unification of mind and body and in this way they must work together.

If the enemy was quick enough to grab your

shoulder with his left hand and pull you and tries to strike your head, you should promptly strike his *Men* with your right fist, parry his right hand with your left fist, then grab his right wrist with both your hands, and by quickly stepping forward with your left foot and turning your body throw the enemy to his rear.

(Usually left is "Yang" and right is "Yin", but in movement it is the other way around.) From ancient times the old saying was that *Bujutsu* was handed down from the gods to the Emperor, and from the Emperor to the commanders.

There is a divine lesson in the truth that all strength consists of movement and stillness, coagulation and loosening, dividing and combining and when this is portrayed wholeheartedly in daily practice to train your body, you can then start to speak of *Budo*.

When the enemy comes to grab your shoulder you must move with the intention of cutting him from *Hasso* diagonally through his shoulder, or of cutting his leg. When he tries to cut your shoulder from *Hasso* or from *Dai-Jodan*, you should invite his sword with the spirit of that very shoulder which is his target and either move forward with your right foot to cut him down, or step back with your left foot to pull him down.

In the old days in *Ken-po* there was a tactic in which you let the enemy cut your skin while you cut his flesh; or letting him cut your flesh, you cut him through the bones. This was a fighting technique where you had to stay calm even under his swiftly cutting sword and cut his flesh just the moment he cuts your skin. Today, however, we deplore even letting him cut our skin.

Even letting someone cut our skin should not be done because it is, after all, dangerous and damaging to the body. You should defeat your enemy without letting it come to that. That is to say, when you lead him with your mind you can defeat him without hurting your body.

Budo should be practiced so that "leading" can be the same as "defeating". The technique of cutting the enemy's flesh while letting him cut your skin is the technique of a master, and is not one to be used by all the Japanese people. In wartime, it is dangerous to make small sacrifices even if it means annihilating the enemy. Real *Bujutsu* is to defeat your enemy without losing even a single man.

Defeat the enemy by securing a safe and undefeatable position. Make them submit without sacrificing a single private of your own. This is a most necessary resolution for your *Budo* training.

Taking this one step further, you have to train enough to have no openings for your enemy to take advantage of.

So, at the instant the enemy grabs your shoulder, you strike his face, move forward with your left foot, grab his right hand and twist, then pin him down to the front; but all of this action should be accomplished by the workings of *Kokoro*. When the mind (*Kokoro*) is manifested in your body, things go along according to *Kokoro*. Here we are training our bodies but the fruit of it all is the training of the mind or spirit (*Kokoro*).

When the enemy comes to grab your shoulder and pull, you act along with this intent (*Kokoro*) and taking advantage of it, thrust [out] your shoulder. All this shows that *Bujutsu* is an expression of mind. As soon as the will to pull the shoulder occurs in the enemy's heart or mind (*Kokoro*), it is necessary for this side to already be aware of that intention (*Kokoro*).

To reiterate, using your mind (*Kokoro*) to lead your enemy to grab your shoulder is one [form of] *Bujutsu*, and if you understand it, overcoming him is easy. But understanding this only with your mind (*Kokoro*) is not enough. You have to understand and realize this truth with your body. That is what can really be called training in *Bujutsu*.

In *Bujutsu* there are shouts like Ei!, Yah!, Toh!, or Ha!. But these are not all; there must be as many as there are words that Japanese people can say.

[In *Kiai*] it is important to project [the voice] like a weapon, as *Kotodama* made up from the unification of voice, mind and rhythm (timing or impulse), in concert with the *Kokyu* of the Universe, and bring together all of these with the physical body. When you begin to unite the voice, body and *Kokoro*, techniques will start to have effect. With the unification of body and soul (*Tamashii*), training and polishing this great power is all the more realizable, and becomes [true] *Bujutsu* practice.

Working this way you can understand how to draw his cut with the sword. The great vigor (or spirit) of *Bujutsu* in this world reaches over the practice site and covers the hearts (*Kokoro*) and bodies [of the trainees]; the more one trains, the more of this spirit is accumulated and you can become a great pillar or *Bujutsu*.

You must devote your whole heart and soul to training, [always] keeping in mind the principle where, in accordance with the grace of the *Kami*, all the *Ki* of *Bujutsu* and the spirits of Yagyu-Jubei, Tsukahara Bokuden and the [other] ancient experts and masters come together.

You must unite with the universal *Kokyu* [and] practice everyday by making you body one with the 'soul of the words', which was given to us human beings. Then in any situation, you [can] cut shouting "Ei!", receive with "Yah!" and break off with "Toh!". Actually, only if both people have the same skill and determination and neither has any openings, can they break off with "Toh!", since if one side has an opening he will cut with "Ei!" [and] "Yah!".

In medieval days, opponents joined [the battle] with "Ei!" and "Yah!", and broke off with "Toh!" and with the [next] "Ei! Yah!" it was finished. In this way they accumulated mutual training in having no *Suki* (openings).

If you reach the point of accumulating a certain amount of enthusiastic, repetitious practice, when the real fight comes, you will see the fallen form of the enemy there, before you even raise a hand. It is [very] interesting to be able to apply a technique and throw him along those lines. You should train with the belief that when you are enthusiastic the techniques come in this way.

4. Munamoto-Dori
(Taking the front of the collar)

As soon as the enemy grabs your collar, you strike his *Men* with your right hand and his left arm with your left hand, then step deeply forward in front of him with your left foot and, pushing with your left shoulder throw him down with feeling.

In principle, being grabbed by the collar is the same as being thrusted at with a spear or stabbed with a sword from *Seigan* [*Kamae*].

There are [two] possibilities: that of the collar [area] being grabbed and pulled, and that of a thrust or a punch. In the first case, being held by the enemy, you must draw the enemy's *Kokoro* in toward yourself, and so leading him, turn ("change") your body. When he comes to punch, you should take advantage of his intention and step back with your left foot, turn you body and throw to your left rear.

When he grabs your collar and attempts to pull, you should give in to this pull and go forward, making him grab and pull still more, then pin him to your own front. You throw him by taking advantage of the unguarded position formed in preparation for the pull by his concentration of force at your collar.

5. Tekubi-o-tsukamu-koto
(Grabbing Wrists)

Wholehearted (*Kokoro*) unification of the hands, feet and *Koshi* (the hip region) is most necessary for defending your mind (*Kokoro*) and body. This especially the case here, because both leading other people and being led by someone are done with the hands. One hand leads and the other throws the enemy down. You have to really understand this. When the enemy wants to pull, first you should cause in him the intention (*Kokoro*) to pull and then make him [actually] try to do so.

As your *Bujutsu* training approaches perfection you will be able to detect the unsatisfactory places [in the enemy's technique], the *Suki*, even before he can and as if to satisfy some deficiency in him, you can apply your technique.

Miyukihime-no-Mikoto[9], daughter of *Susanoo-no-Mikoto* was full of encouragement for *Bu* and as a result many heroes gathered under her. Suspecting that she might start something with all these warriors around, the other gods sent down a brigade of celestial soldiers. But having no intention of fighting against these troops, she opened up the castle gates and led them inside, giving them the warmest of receptions and made peace [with them].

True *Budo* is practiced not only to destroy an enemy, it must also make him, of his own will, gladly lose his spirit (*Seishin*) to oppose you.

True *Budo* is done for the sake of 'building peace'. Train every day so as to make peace between this spirit [of *Budo*] and all things manifested on the face of the earth.

If your opponent comes to grab your wrist, step back with your left foot and lead him with the hand he seeks to take and with your other hand strike down onto his neck.

In China they teach that when something dies it [simply] ceases to be, whereas in Japan we believe that though something should die, it not only does not cease, it actually flourishes. You have to be determined to carry out your original intention to the end. Above all, a person who trains in Bujutsu should come to understand the principle of *Ikidoshi* ('the Flow of Life'). In Japanese *Bujutsu* all the teachings of the Universe are spelled out. For example, even when being surrounded by countless spears you should see them as one person as they thrust. It is a mistake to use pillars or trees and shrubs as a shield like the warriors of old. Stand right in front of the advancing enemy with his intention (*Kokoro*) [to attack] as your shield; enter into the center of the thrusting spears and, utilizing the principle of "turning the body" (*Tenkan*), break out their enclosure to safety without any trouble. In this way, even if you are completely surrounded by the enemy, you must move against them form an undefeatable posture (or attitude) based on the principle of IRIMI TENKAN.

There is an old Chinese adage that says you should be willing to die for the sake of the people who truly understand you. But this is a foreign thought, not Japanese. It may be true in China, but in Japan your body is your own and at the same time not only yours. It was given by the gods which is the same as saying it is the Emperor's. Since it is the Emperor's, you cannot selfishly kill yourself just as you please. Therefore, dying for somebody who understands you is contrary to native Japanese ideas and is a Chinese thought which came to Japan with Confucianism.

One should repay his debt to the Emperor in all sincerity even if other people do not know it. Therefore, as long as even one arm is functioning as an arm it must be treated with care, [as the property of the Emperor]. Even small teachings like this are manifested in Japanese *Bujutsu*.

Since to defeat your enemy is [the method of] *Bujutsu* training, you should practice to embody the above reasoning and truth(s). Fight masses of the enemy as if they were one man, and deal with one enemy as if he were many; this is the way you must do battle. Move in such a way that without any *Suki* (openings) you make one [principle] fit the myriad of [possibilities]. Training done not only for the purpose of cutting each other, but also for governing the universe is [true] *Bujutsu* practice.

It is necessary to build up sincerity of a *Yamatodamashii* that is without openings in either mind or body; and to train to defeat your enemy with your spirit (*Kokoro*) whether he strikes you from *Jo-Dan*, *Chu-Dan* or *Ge-Dan*, from the front or back, or the right or left, using the faithful *Irimi-Tenkan* principle of *Aiki*. No matter what kind of terrible crisis should occur, even if the whole world turns against you, this spiritual technique is enough to pull you through. You must never let down your guard! (Lit.: Never loosen [your] *Kokoro*).

Build god's (*Kami*) mind (*Kokoro*) inside Man's physical body. Like the light that pierces the darkness, you must discipline [yourself] with ever deepening *Keiko*.

In an ancient text written to record the secret principles of *Bujutsu* it is written that *Bujutsu* must become like sunlight. "When a door (*fusuma*) is opened, who can say when it came in?" But I do not agree. This light should be able to shine through *Fusuma*, a wall, a rock or anything! Otherwise it is a mistake to call it Japanese *Bujutsu*.

1 **Aite**: opponent, training partner.

2 **Kyori**: distance, spacing. Often used to mean Maai, a technical word meaning ' combative engagement distance'.

3 **Kendo**: This term was often used very loosely and did not imply the modern sport form as popularized today, but referred to older concepts perhaps more correctly called *Kenjutsu*.

4 **Suigetsu**: written with the characters for water (*sui*) and moon (*getsu*). This term also means the solar plexis, or the pit of the stomach. The principle of *Suigetsu* is an important but very cryptic idea related to instant response to the opponent's movement.

5 **Iwato-biraki-no-gyo**: literally means "to achieve the opening of the Great Door of Stone". This expression comes from the *Kojiki*, one of Japan's oldest semi-historical texts, which is revered as the main repository of the ancient myths of Shinto. One famous story tells of the Sungoddess, ancestor of the Imperial line, who hid herself in a cave after being insulted by one other of the Kami. Since she had sealed herslef in with a huge boulder no sunlight could escape to the earth, threatening the destruction of all life there.

In order to prevent this disaster the other gods arranged for a suggestive dance to be performed in front of the cave. Upon hearing the noisy exicitement outside, the curious goddess cracked the door to take a peak at the dance and a male diety of great strength was then able to push back the great stone door and restore the light of the sun to the world.

O-Sensei uses the story symbolically to illustrate the ultimate goal of training, which he calls 'the opening of the great stone door of the spirit'. Through protracted, diligent *Keiko* one is able to put his physical and spiritual sides into harmony, or as Mr. Takahashi Hideo relates in his book *Takemusu Aiki*, to 'make the body and soul parallel', for the purpose of 'illuminating the world of the spirit'. The personal *Iwato-birki-no-gyo* is called a return to the true nature of the soul' just as the reappearance of the Sungoddess restored its original condition to the created world.

O-Sensei immersed himself in the lore of Shinto and often spoke of the various *Kami*, using them to expand his explanations of the techniques and goals of Aikido. However, even most Japanese have little knowledge of these legends and their meaning and it seems few were able to comprehend exactly what it was the master was trying to say.

6 **Ki**: spirit, mind, soul, heart, intention, mood, feeling; or, air, atmosphere, energy, essence.

7 **Ken-po**: literally the "Law of the Sword"; sword method.

8 **Hasso**: a *Kamae*, or combative posture where the weapon is held over one shoulder beside the head ready to strike.

9 **Susanoo-no-Mikoto, Miyukihime-no Mikoto**: both Shinto dieties; *Susanoo* was the Sungoddess' younger brother.

USHIRO-WAZA (Rear Techniques)

Ushiro-dori demands that you train yourself in *Bujutsu* until your body, soul (*Tamashii*) and the five senses work as a single, integrated personality. The goal is to use intuition when moving your mind against the rear. Whenever an enemy comes to grab you from the rear, you should open onto your whole body the window of the spirit (*Kokoro*) which has eyes facing even to the rear. Your back must move instantly and vigorously with soul and body unified in response to the unexpected attack.

Grabbing from the rear is very dangerous even for the one who is attacking. That is because in making a 'surprise' attack, chances are high that somewhere his own mind (*Kokoro*) has been left unguarded. Therefore he may suffer an unexpected defeat. This point calls for particular care. Even though your enemy may be facing the other way, if his skill is greater than yours, his body will always be full of the spirit of *Bujutsu*, even to the rear, and it will be dangerous [for you to attack him]. When being grabbed from the rear, turn your body to the right or left and promptly take him on. [To accomplish this] it is necessary to gain training experience until you are able to take him off-balance when you turn your body. These techniques are done to develop vigorous powers of intuition. The back of a human body is made so as to move spiritually when doing *Bujutsu*. Therefore, you should train hard every day to make your intuition keener. When this is accomplished, as the enemy comes to grab you from the rear you can defeat him by simply stepping forward.

USHIRO-ERI (Back of the Collar)

Being grabbed be the rear collar incorporates the same principle as when an enemy standing behind you tries cutting straight down from *Jo-Dan* with his sword. In the case of a woman, it is the same as being pulled down by the hair. When being grabbed by the rear collar, promptly turn your body and strike his face, or his *Men* and *Suigetsu*, in order to crush his spirit and open his spiritual window. In any fight where an enemy comes to attack you from the rear, promptly turn (*Tenkan*) your body toward him and change your position to punch the right (or left) side of his head. Or spin your body and go in directly behind him and attack from the right rear. Train to strengthen and unify your hip movement. If, in *Ushiro-dori*, when you strike your enemy's *Men* he grabs that hand, promptly turn your body by stepping back with your left foot and throw him by cutting down to the right or by stepping back with your right foot to his left.

The above explanation covers only a small fraction of all the possible techniques, and since there is only a limited number of pages in this book, the details of each technique and the secret of *Hei-Do*[1] (*Sen-Do*)[2] behind them all will be laid out at the proper time during actual practice.

1 **Hei-Do**: （兵道） literally "the Way of the Soldier".
2 **Sen-Do**: （戦道） literally "the Way of War".

Technical Illustrations and Explanations

SUWARI-WAZA (Sitting Techniques)

Shomen (Front or Face on)

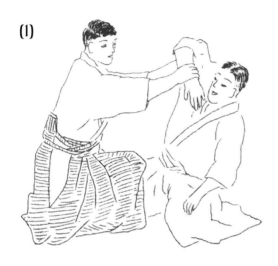

1. *Shi*: (Black *Hakama*): Using the right hand, strikes for the face of his opponent and with his left hand thrusts to the armpit at the same time raising his body (*Koshi*) [to *Kiza* position].

Uke: (White *Hakama*): With his own right hand blocks *Shi*'s right handed attack.

Shi: At the same time as grasping his enemy's right hand moves slightly forward on his left knee and pulling down his own right hand uses his left to suppress *Uke*'s elbow.

2. *Uke*: Strikes out with his right hand and at the same time punches with his left.

Shi: Using his right hand to receive the enemy's right strike simultaneously steps back to his right rear and with his left hand grasping *Uke*'s right elbow, pins it downward to his own right.

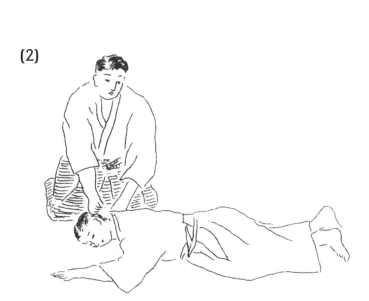

(1)

(2)

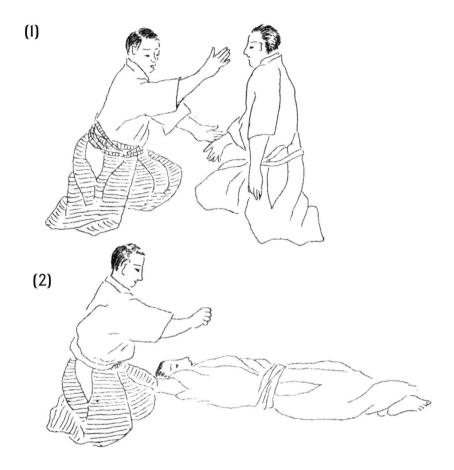

Yokomen (Side of the Head [strike])

3. *Uke*: Attacks his partner's *Yokomen* using his right hand.

Shi: Moves resolutely to the left on his left knee and at the same time intercepts *Uke*'s right hand with his own left hand and cuts down the enemy's *Yokomen* with a right handed strike.

(1)

Kata (Shoulder)

4. *Uke*: Grasps *Shi*'s left shoulder with his right hand.

Shi: Strikes *Shomen* (the face) with his right hand and *Uke*'s right elbow with his left hand. While doing so, *Shi* advances on his left knee, and grasping *Uke*'s right hand with his own right pushes down in a forward direction.

(2)

(3)

Sode (Sleeve)

5. *Uke*: Grasps his partner's left sleeve with his right hand.

Shi: At the same time as he is grabbed [by *Uke*] strikes *Shomen* with his right hand and moves obliquely to the left, using his left hand to strike down *Uke*'s right elbow.

(1)

(2)

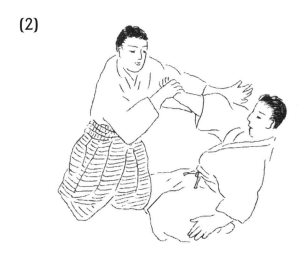

(1)

6. *Uke*: With his left hand grasps his partner's right sleeve and strikes out with his right hand.

Shi: Receives the attacking right hand with his own right and as [his own right knee] touches [the mat after moving slightly to the right] strikes *Uke* down with his left hand into a face-up position.

(2)

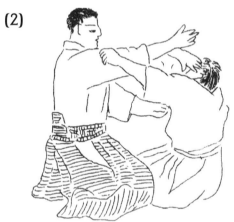

(3)

Ryosode (Both Sleeves)

7. *Uke*: Holds both of *Aite*'s sleeves.

Shi: Striking *Shomen* (the face) with his right hand and the enemy's right elbow with his left, takes *Uke*'s right hand in his own right hand and strikes down in a forward direction (This is the same as No. 4).

(1)

(2)

(3)

(1)

Mune (Chest)

8. *Uke*: Grasps *Aite*'s chest with his right hand.

Shi: Standing up onto his toes [in the *Kiza* position], strikes *Men* (the face or head) with his right and simultaneously moves forward on his left knee and opens his body to the right.

(2)

(3)

(1)

9. *Uke*: Grasping *Aite*'s collar area with his left hand and strikes out with his right.

Shi: Striking around from the outside with the right hand, receives and grasps the oncoming [right hand] and with his left takes hold of the hand [clinging] to his throat, [then] crossing them in an "X" shape thrusts downward in a forward direction.

(2)

(1)

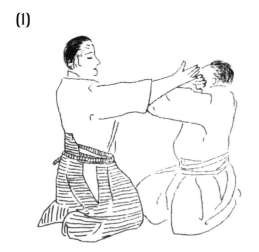

10. ([*Shi* may also] bring his right hand around *Uke*'s extended left arm and grasp *Uke*'s right handed *Men* attack [as in No. 9], then strike to the body: or, leaving *Uke*'s left hand at his throat [use the trapped right hand as a lever] to push *Uke*'s right elbow down onto *Uke*'s own extended left elbow.)

(2)

Kubijime (Choke or Strangle Hold)

11. Uke: Grasps *Aite*'s lapels in a crossed fashion [right hand on left lapel, left hand on right lapel] (with his right hand on top).

Shi: Drawing back on his right knee and striking *Men* (face) inserts his left hand from below and placing it on *Uke*'s left arm, twists *Uke*'s head by applying his hand underneath [*Uke*'s chin] and his right hand from above [*Uke*'s head].

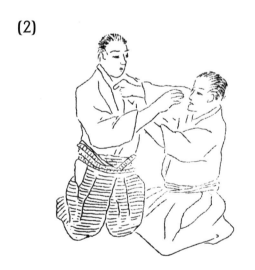

(3)

(4)

(1)

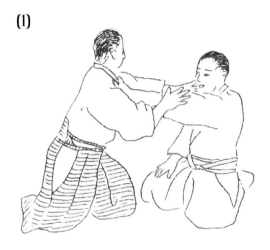

12. *Uke*: Same as above [in No. 11 but with his left hand only].

Shi: Inserting his left hand from below, pins [by] cutting downward from his enemy's left shoulder to [his own] right.

(2)

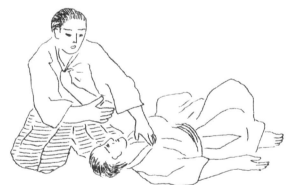

(1)

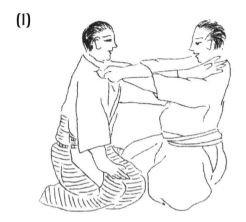

13. *Uke*: Grasps as before and twists [his hands to choke].

Shi: Strikes *Men* with his right hand and inserts his left hand [between *Uke*'s extended arms] and cuts down the enemy's left shoulder.

(2)

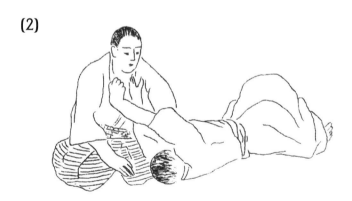

(1)

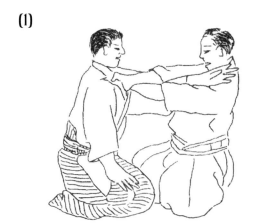

14. *Uke*: Same as before.

Shi: Applying his left hand from above *Uke*'s left arm [by passing the arms], grasps his own [left] wrist with his right hand.

(2)

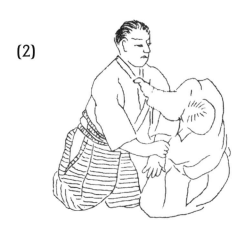

(3)

(1)

Te (Hand)

15. *Uke*: Grasps both of his partner's hands with both of his hands. [*Ryotedori*]

Shi: Turning his palms inward enough that the hands are in a standing position with the thumbs visible, puts his power into his finger tips and pushes [*Uke*] down straight [back] away from himself. When pinning to the left the right hand must be sufficiently extended [and vice versa].

(2)

(3)

(1)

16. *Uke*: Same as [No. 15,] above.

Shi: By putting strength into his fingers and raising them in a fashion that draws *Uke* in [toward himself] advances with his right knee and throws [*Uke*] over his head to the rear.

(2)

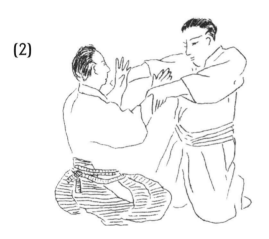

(3)

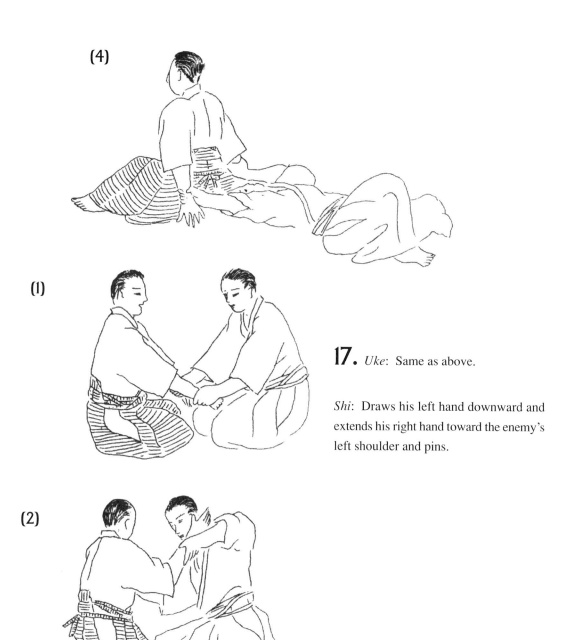

17. *Uke*: Same as above.

Shi: Draws his left hand downward and extends his right hand toward the enemy's left shoulder and pins.

18. *Uke*: [Grasping] in the same manner as before pushes downward toward *Shi*'s knees.

Shi: Sticks his right hand to his right knee and pulls [that leg back] and, at the same time, [continues that *kuzushi* movement by] putting *Uke*'s left hand on top of his right knee, frees his own right hand and strikes *Men*.

(1)

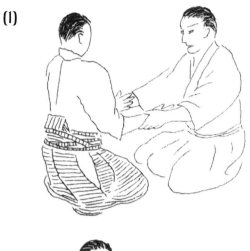

19. *Uke*: Grasps both of his *Aite*'s hands with both of his own hands and pushes.

Shi: Withdrawing his right knee and facing both hands upward carries [*Uke*] to the right.

(2)

(1)

20. *Uke*: Same as above.

Shi: Forcefully puts his right hand onto his enemy's right elbow and pushing there, takes [away] his left hand and strikes *Men*, throwing him down [to *Uke*'s own right rear.]

(2)

(3)

(4)

(1)

21. *Uke*: Same as above.

Shi: Facing his palms up extends straight out and throws to *Uke*'s left [or right].

(2)

(3)

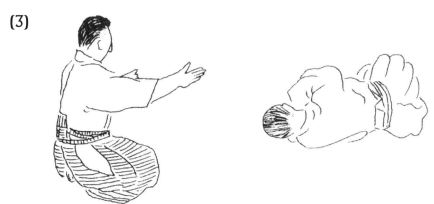

(1)

22. *Uke*: Same as before.

Shi: Placing his right hand onto *Uke*'s right hand from above, slips in to *Uke*'s right flank breaking [his left hand] free from *Uke*'s right hand. Then drawing his right knee back around, *Shi* grasps *Uke*'s left sleeve and [pulls, causing *Uke* to take a front *Ukemi*] then pins [*Uke*'s left arm across his face].

(2)

(3)

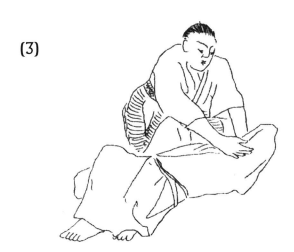

Hanmi-Handachi (Half Sitting Half Standing)

(1)

23. *Uke*: Approaching from *Shi*'s right side takes *Shi*'s right hand in his own left hand and strikes out with his right fist.

Shi: While moving on his right knee in the same direction that he is being pulled raises his right hand obliquely [toward his center front] and grasping *Uke*'s left wrist with his left hand raises it over his head. With his own hands held as if glued to his head, *Shi* turns to his left and strikes down and pins.

(2)

(3)

(4)

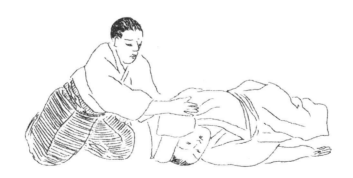

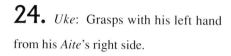

24. *Uke*: Grasps with his left hand from his *Aite*'s right side.

Shi: Advances to *Uke*'s rear on his right knee and takes down his enemy's left knee with his right elbow. [Then] grasping *Uke*'s left ankle with his left hand, controls.

(1)

25. *Uke*: Grasping *Shi*'s right hand as before, strikes out [with his right hand].

Shi: At the instant the strike comes, advances to the left front on his right knee and thrusts outward toward the lower right front with his right hand.

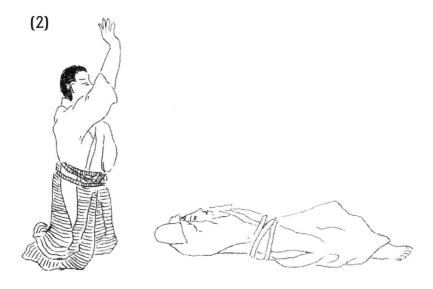

(2)

26. *Uke*: Same as above [in No. 25].

Shi: Pushing his right hand to *Uke*'s rear and moving to the right on his right knee, uses his left hand to sweep *Uke*'s [leading] left foot forward [for the throw].

(1)

(2)

(3)

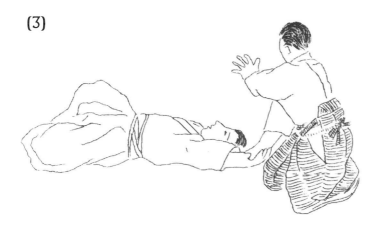

(1)

27. *Uke*: Same as above [two techniques].

Shi: Wielding his right hand upward over his head, and turning it from right to left around the rear, strikes [*Uke*] down to his own left front.

(2)

(3)

(1)

28. *Uke*: Same as above.

Shi: At the same time as swinging his right hand upward, stands his right leg up toward the right front and moving slightly in that direction, grasps *Uke*'s left wrist with his left hand; while standing up he turns and cuts [*Uke*] down to the left.

(2)

(3)

(4)

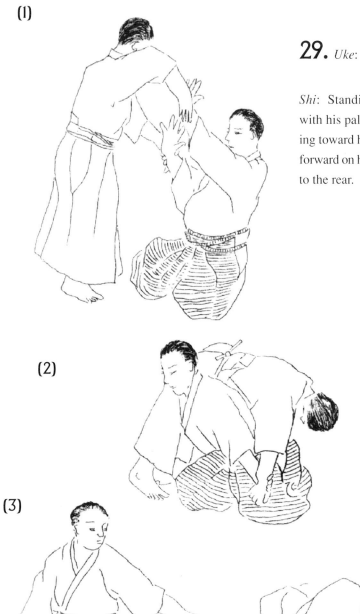

29. *Uke*: Grasps both wrists from the front.

Shi: Standing up on his toes [*Kiza* posture] with his palms facing inward and while pulling toward himself and lifting, steps obliquely forward on his right foot to throw over his head to the rear.

30. *Uke*: Same as above [No. 29].

Shi: Inching forward on his right knee, grabs his enemy's left ankle with his left hand and takes *Uke*'s left knee with his right; then pushes and pins. (Instead of grasping the knee, a striking attack and pin are also possible.)

(1)

(2)

(3)
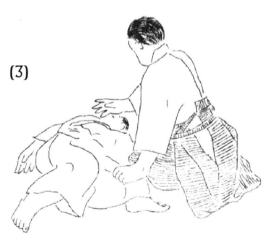

31. *Uke*: Same as above. [*Ryotedori*]

(1)

Shi: Grasps the attacker's left wrist with his own left hand and pulls to [his own] left [while advancing on his right knee]. Then, freeing his right hand [*Shi*] strikes [*Uke*'s] face.

[Note: The hands in the second drawing seem to be misdrawn.]

(2)

(1)

32. *Uke*: Same as above.

Shi: Raises both hands with the palms facing inward while standing up on his left foot [into *Tatehiza* position] then advances forward between *Uke*'s legs, lowers his hands beginning with the right and throws over his head to the rear.

(2)

(1)

(2)

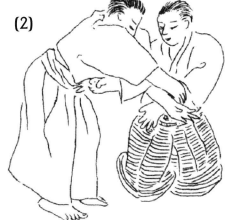

33. *Uke*: Same as above.

Shi: Putting his left hand on top of *Uke*'s left, slips in to *Uke*'s left side to free his right hand. Then, after punching the body, he pulls [*Uke*'s] right sleeve and cuts [down and] throws.

(3)

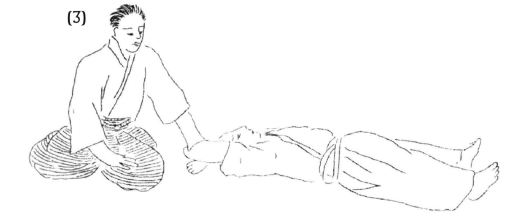

34. *Uke*: Same as above.

Shi: Moves his left hand to his own lower left and sending strength into his right palm thrusts it out in the direction of the enemy's left shoulder; [then] advancing on his right leg [and turning his body] he cuts down and throws obliquely to the left.

(1)

(2)

35. *Uke*: Same as above.

Shi: Simultaneously grasping the enemy's left hand with his left and thrusting out with his right, raises them up to his head [in sword fashion] and raises [his body up] onto his right foot and left toes. [Then] turning to the front and standing up, *Shi* continues turning and throws to the rear.

[Note: Picture No. 4 is drawn from a different angle.]

TACHI-WAZA (Standing Techniques)

(1)

(2)

Shomen (Front of Face on)

36. *Shi*: Strikes out with his right *Tegatana* (Hand blade) and with his left hand thrusts to the enemy's right arm pit.

Uke: Receives this attack with his right hand.

Shi: Advancing on his right leg and stepping in with his left foot, grabs the enemy's right elbow with his left hand. (You must put your strength into your finger tips.)

(3)

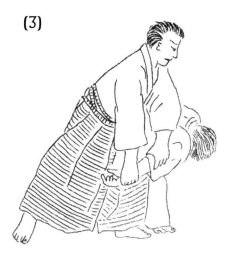

(1)

37. *Uke*: Strikes out with his right hand.

Shi: At the instant *Uke* swings up his hand, receives the attack with the feeling of entering [using the right hand]. Then, grasping *Uke*'s right arm, *Shi* opens his body by drawing his right leg around and pulls [*Uke*] down.

(2)

(1)

38. *Uke*: Strikes with his right hand.

Shi: Swinging his right leg around [to his rear], cuts down the enemy's right hand with his left [then] punches *Men* with his right. Regrasping *Uke*'s right wrist with his own right hand, *Shi* extends his left hand and cuts down across the front of *Uke*'s neck.

[Note: Picture No. 1 shows only the initial *Ai-Gamae*]

(2)

(3)

(4)

(1)

39. *Uke*: Same as above.

Shi: Drawing his right leg and cutting down the enemy's right hand [as before], pushes the enemy's chin with his right hand and advances again on his right leg.

(2)

(3)

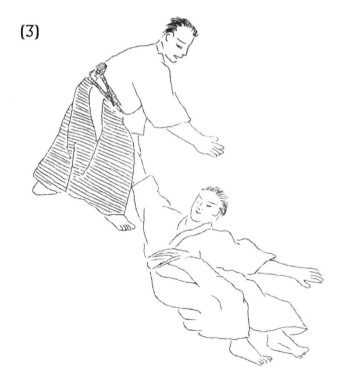

40. *Uke*: Same as above.

Shi: Takes a big step back with his left foot and cutting downward on the opponent's neck with his right hand throws him down to *Uke*'s own front. (With this one, pulling his right hand or sleeve with your left hand is also effective.)

(1)

(2)

(3)

(4)

(1)

41. *Uke*: Same as above [i.e. a right-handed *Shomen Uchi*].

Shi: Blocking ('receiving') with his right hand, advances forward one step on his left foot and thrusts with his left hand to the enemy's ribs.

Yokomen (Side of the Head [strike])

(1)

42. *Uke*: Strikes *Yokomen* with his right hand.

Shi: Advancing to the left with his left foot, uses his left hand to cut down and grab *Uke*'s [attacking] right hand, then chops down onto the enemy' neck with his right hand.

[Note: Picture No. 1 shows the initial *Kamae* only.]

(2)

(1)

43. *Uke*: Same as before.

Shi: Steps forward on his right foot at the instant [*Uke*] raises [his hand] then steps with his left foot toward the enemy's right rear [corner] pushing his chin with his left hand.

(2)

44. *Uke*: Same as before.

Shi: Receiving with his left hand and pulling his left foot, strikes *Men* with his right. Then grasping the enemy's right hand with both of his own, *Shi* encroaches deeply upon [*Uke*'s space] with his left foot, and [turning], cuts him down while advancing with his right foot.

(2)

(3)

(4)

(1)

45. *Uke*: Same as before [i.e. a right handed *Yokomen Uchi* attack].

Shi: Drawing his right foot [back] and receiving [the attack] with his left hand, again pulls the right leg to the rear, turns underneath and throws as in the previous Kata, [No. 44].

(2)

(3)

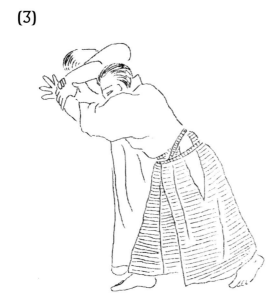

(1)

(2)-1

46. *Uke*: Same as above.

Shi: Draws his left foot back and cuts down [the attack] with his right hand, then advancing again on his left foot to the enemy's rear takes hold of *Uke*'s right wrist from beneath with his own right hand, extends his left hand and catches up the enemy's neck in his left armpit. (Or [as in Picture No. 2, *Shi* may] grasp the enemy's right hand with his own right hand and turn [it] to the front, then bringing his left hand around from behind the enemy, [re]grasp *Uke*'s right hand and use his [now freed] right to pull and suppress the enemy's right elbow, [pinning across *Uke*'s face].

(2)-2

47. *Uke*: Same as above.

Shi: At the same time as he draws his left foot back, drops down onto his left knee and strikes the enemy's left armpit [side] with his right hand; then using his left, he grabs *Uke*'s right sleeve to pull and throw.

(1)

(2)

(1)

48. *Uke*: Same as before.

Shi: Moves his body leftward as he moves out on his left foot to the left and entering there, in *Hanmi* ('half-body') posture, throws to the left with both hands.

(2)

Kata (Shoulder [grabbed])

49. *Uke*: Grasps his *Aite*'s left shoulder and pulls, using his right hand.

Shi: Strikes *Men* with his right hand, and grasping the enemy's right hand advances on his left foot in such a way as to push outward with his left shoulder; then grasping the enemy's right elbow with his left hand, pins to the front.

(1)

50. *Uke*: Grasps *Shi*'s right shoulder with his left hand.

Shi: Advancing from his left foot, steps in to the enemy's rear with his right leg and extends his right elbow toward the front of the enemy's neck.

(2)

(1)

51. *Uke*: Grasp his *Aite*'s right shoulder with his left hand and strikes out [at *Men*] with his right.

Shi: Receiving [the blow] with his left and stepping forward between his enemy's legs, bends his head down deeply and throws over his head to the rear.

[Note: *Shi*'s right handed *Atemi* to *Uke*'s face in Picture No. 1.]

(2)

(1)

52. *Uke*: Grasps *Aite*'s right shoulder with his left hand and strikes Yokomen with his right.

Shi: Receives with his left and strikes *Men* with his right; then, grasping the enemy's right hand with both hands, advances under it on his left foot and throws to the front.

(2)

(3)

(1)

53. *Uke*: Holds *Aite*'s right shoulder with his left hand.

Shi: Grasps *Uke*'s right hand with his right and strikes *Men* with his left; then advancing on his left foot and turning under [*Uke*'s arm] to put *Uke*'s right hand onto his own right shoulder, grabs the back of *Uke*'s collar with his left hand and pulls.

(2)

54. Proceed as in technique 53 but after grabbing the back of the collar overcome him by drawing the left foot back again.

(1)

55. *Uke*: Holding as before, now strikes with his right hand.

Shi: Moving on his right foot to the enemy's right side [i.e. to his own left], catches the right elbow [with his left hand] and pushing forward with his right hand on the enemy' chin, cuts him down.

(2)

56. *Uke*: Attacks as before.

Shi: Receives with his left hand and changes his grip [on the attacking arm] to his right hand, and , while taking one step forward with his left foot, pulls the right arm to his own right rear. Then, releasing his right hand, *Shi* wraps it around the enemy's neck and stepping into the enemy's right rear, pushes him down toward his on front.

(3)

(1)

57. *Uke*: Same as before.

Shi: Receiving with his left hand and at the same time taking a big step back with his left foot, sticks out his right shoulder toward the front and drops to his left knee. Then pulling his left hand, he pulls [*Uke*] down toward the front [sweeping *Uke*'s right foot with his right hand.]

(2)

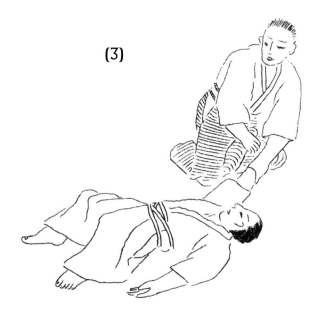

(3)

(1)

58. *Uke*: Same as before.

Shi: Striking *Men* with his right and grasping *Uke*'s right hand in his left, draws his left foot back around and turns [to face] the rear.

(2)

59. *Uke*: Grabs as before [with his left at *Shi*'s right shoulder] but now pulls and strikes with his right hand.

Shi: Striking *Men* with his left, enters to the enemy's left side by advancing on his right foot. Then turning to the right, he extends his right arm in front of *Uke* and steps in behind him with his right leg throwing him to the right rear.

Note: Enter under *Uke*'s left arm.

(3)

(1)

60. *Uke*: Attacks as before.

Shi: Advancing on his right foot, inserts only the upper half of his body under the enemy's left armpit; then taking hold of *Uke*'s *Obi* (belt) at his left [*Uke*'s right rear], *Shi* pushes *Uke*'s *Koshi* (hip region) with his right hand and throws to [his own] left rear. (Here it is also possible to advance on the left foot and enter under the enemy's right armpit.)

(2)

(3)

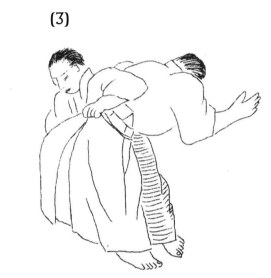

Sode (Sleeve)

61. *Uke*: Takes hold of his *Aite*'s right sleeve with his left hand and pulls.

Shi: Advances in the direction he is being pulled while pushing *Uke*'s [left] elbow up with both Tegatana. then using his left hand to grasp *Uke*'s left hand and advancing to the front on his right foot, *Shi* uses his right hand to cut down onto [*Uke*'s left] elbow.

(3)

62. *Uke*: Uses his left hand to grasp the right sleeve of his *Aite* and then attacks [*Men*] using his right.

Shi: Turning his right hand from the inside, grasps his enemy's left sleeve and drawing his right leg around to the rear drops to his right knee. [Though not expressly stated, Picture No. 2 makes it appear that *Shi* stepped into *Uke*'s right front with his left leg before swinging his right foot around.]

(1)

63. *Uke*: [grips and attacks] as before [in 62].

Shi: Receives with his right hand and continuing in the same movement wraps [*Uke*'s right hand] around [*Uke*'s own left arm from above]. then pulling *Uke*'s left sleeve with his left hand, *Shi* draws his right foot out and drops to his right knee which pulls [*Uke*] down.

(2)

(3)

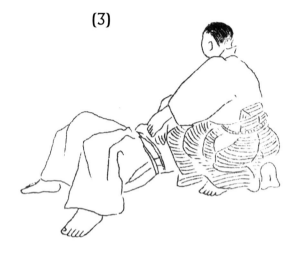

64. *Uke*: Same as above, [grasping *Shi*'s right shoulder and striking *Men* with his right hand].

Shi: Steps to the left with his left foot and receiving with his right hand, puts strength into his finger tips and stretches his right hand out from *Uke*'s neck. [Then] wrapping [his right hand] around [*Uke*'s neck] with his palm facing to the outside, and grabbing and pulling the back of *Uke*'s collar with his left hand, *Shi* step in again to *Uke*'s rear on his right foot. [This final stepping action is not illustrated.] (Or receiving the attack with his right, but unable to step in with his right foot, *Shi* grabs *Uke*'s left sleeve with his left hand and pulls down behind his right leg.)

65. *Uke*: Using his left hand to grasp *Shi*'s right sleeve, strikes with his right hand [to the face].

Shi: Putting strength into his *Koshi* (hips) steps back on his right leg; then, using the right hand which has been grasped [by the sleeve], suppresses the enemy's attacking right hand and with his left hand grabs the enemy's right sleeve and pulls.

(1)

66. *Uke*: Grasps his *Aite*'s right sleeve with his left hand.

Shi: Using his right foot to advance in behind *Uke*' [left], strikes the face with his right elbow and grabs the enemy's [right] hand with his left.

(2)

(1)

67. *Uke*: Attacks the same as before.

Shi: Simultaneously applies his right hand to *Uke*'s arm from the top and turns deeply around to the rear with his left foot. Next, he again pulls the right foot to the rear.

(Note: Picture No. 2 shows the deep pulling [to the rear] with the left foot.)

(2)

(3)

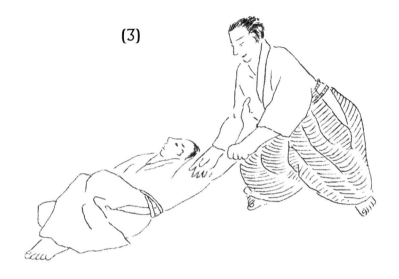

(1)

68. *Uke*: Attacking in the same way as before, *Uke* now pulls as well.

Shi: If pulled, *Shi* must advance on his right foot and strike to the enemy's chest with his right hand. Then raising up his right hand [under *Uke*'s left armpit] and grasping the back of the enemy's collar with his left hand, he punches the body (*Do*) with the right hand and kicks up to *Uke*'s solar plexis (*Mizoochi*) with right foot, and pushes. (It is also possible to draw the left leg back to the rear [as in Picture No. 2 and throw as in Picture No. 3].)

[Note: Picture No. 1 shows only the initial *Kamae*, the first technique is not illustrated.]

(2)

69. *Uke*: Strikes as before.

Shi: Moving his body outward to the right on his right foot and striking the enemy's face with his left hand, applies his right hand to the attacking arm [*Uke*'s left] then passes his head under it and pushes to the front grasping the elbow with his left hand.

(2)

(In this case, if you enter boldly without passing under the attacking [left arm] and punch up to the groin or the back of the knee, it is effective. [But] this means you must lower your head deeply.)

(3)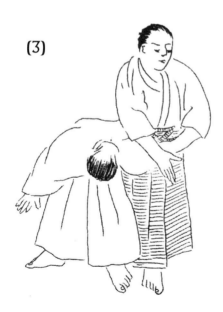

(1)

70. *Uke*: Takes hold with the same grip as before [except with the other hand] and pulls.

Shi: Moves out to the enemy's rear with his right foot simultaneously [with the attack], and while striking *Men* with his right hand, steps again with his right leg and advances deeply to the enemy's rear.

(2)

71. *Uke*: Makes the same attack as above in 70.

Shi: Frees [himself] by advancing on his left leg, passing under the enemy's arm and with his right hand, punches to the armpit (*Waki*) and with his left, thrusts to the hips (*Koshi*). Then he steps out to the front of the enemy on his right leg.

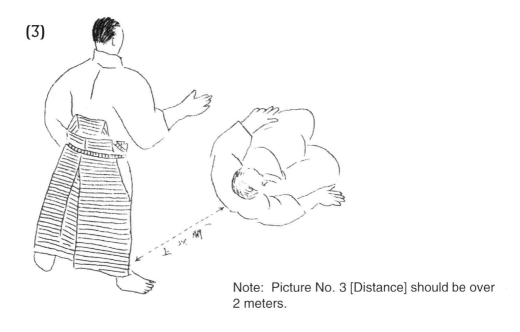

Note: Picture No. 3 [Distance] should be over 2 meters.

72. *Uke*: Grips *Shi*'s right sleeve with his left hand and thrusts at him with his right hand.

Shi: Pulls back deeply with his left foot and "hangs" his right hand onto the enemy's [left] elbow from above.

Note: Picture No. 2 shows pulling the left leg.

(1)

73. *Uke*: Grips *Shi*'s right shoulder with his left hand and punches with his right.

Shi: Using his right foot to step onto the enemy's left foot, brings his right hand around from the outside and down on top of *Uke*'s [left] elbow and pulls his left leg to the rear.

(2)

(3)

(1)

74. *Uke*: Same as above.

Shi: Grabs the oncoming punch with his left hand, then thrusting out his right shoulder, puts the caught arm onto it so that the enemy's hand which is holding his sleeve is now [barred] across his back. Then pushing out his right shoulder at an angle to the front he [can] push and throw.

75. *Uke*: Same as above.

Shi: Turns his right arm around from the inside and grasp his enemy's [left] sleeve. [Then putting] his right foot behind the *Uke*, he steps in again with the other foot and pushes *Uke*'s chin with his left hand.

76. *Uke*: Strikes as above.

Shi: Uses his left hand to punch the body (*Do*) and while stepping back on his right foot, swings his right hand around from the top to grab and pull the enemy's left sleeve.

(2)

([If] you swing your right hand around from above and advance to the front with your left leg, *Koshi Nage* is also good, [but you must] lower your head deeply and insert you left leg between the enemy's feet.)

(3)

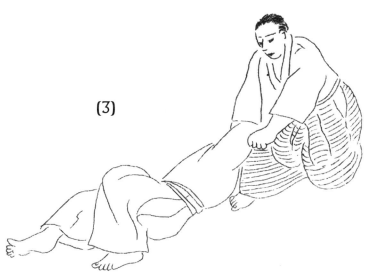

Kata (Shoulders)

77. *Uke*: Uses both hands to grasp both of his *Aite*'s shoulders.

Shi: Punches the face with his left hand and advances with his right foot pointing to the outside [*Tomoe* foot work]; then thrusting the upper half of his body directly in between and up under the enemy's arms, *Shi* steps in to *Uke*'s rear with his left leg. Now, he attacks his enemy's stomach or sides with his elbow.

(3)

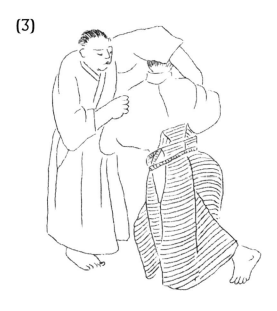

(4)

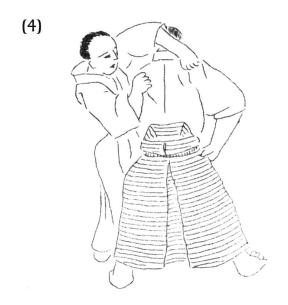

(1)

78. *Uke*: Grasps both of *Aite*'s shoulders and pulls.

Shi: Immediately strikes the face. Simultaneously raising both hands he inserts them from the outside toward the center, over *Uke*'s arms, and ducks his head down deeply; stepping forward between the enemy's legs on his right foot, he then grabs *Uke*'s right leg and springs it up [and over his back].

(2)

79. *Uke*: Same as before.

Shi: Advancing quickly with his right foot behind *Uke*'s back and his left foot in front, *Shi* at the same time swings his right hand from the outside over *Uke*'s [extended] arms and pushes it across the front of his neck, then finishes by grasping *Uke*'s *Obi* at the front.

80. *Uke*: Same as before.

Shi: Strikes *Men* with his right hand and draws his [left] shoulder deeply outside [by] stepping his left foot in to *Uke*'s [right] rear side. Ducking his head down under [*Uke*'s right] arm, he then attacks at the chin [from below] pushing it back and steps in behind with his right foot.

(2)

(3)

Te (Hands), Katate (One Hand)

81. *Uke*: Grasps *Shi*'s right wrist in his left hand and attacks.

Shi: Puts strength into the place where he is being held and with great speed steps in behind *Uke* with his left foot and at the same time raises up his right hand [towards *Uke*'s face], then again advances, now on his right foot [to throw].

(1)

82. *Uke*: Same as above.

Shi: Draws his right foot deeply back at the very instant he is grabbed and strikes for *Uke*'s ribs with his left hand. (*Shi* may also grasp the enemy's left sleeve with his left hand or strike the neck with his left hand.)

(2)

(3)

(1)

Aikinage

83. *Uke*: Same as before.

Shi: At the instant he is pulled, must move in with the pull, and advance on his right foot to the enemy's left front; then at the same time, thrust his right arm out along with the foot in that same direction.

(2)

(3)

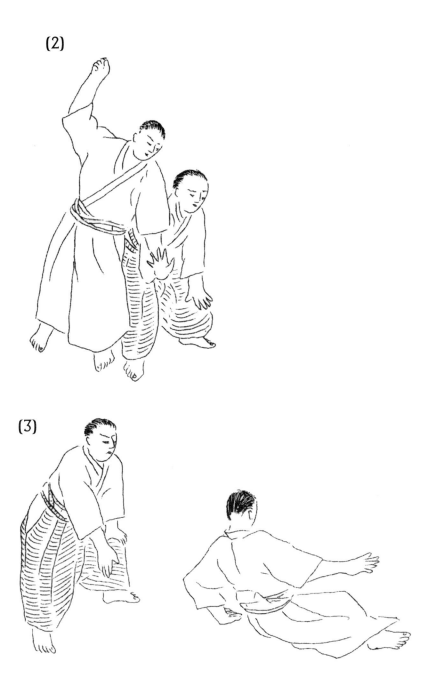

(1)

84. *Uke*: Makes the same attack.

Shi: Turns his right hand around from the outside and sticks it to the enemy's wrist from above, and drawing his left foot around deeply [to the rear] throws [with the same type of *Aikinage* as in No. 83].

(2)

(1)

(2)

85. *Uke*: Same as before [i.e. *Katatedori Shomen Uchi*].

Shi: Attacks the enemy's face and while doing so, slips under his gripping left arm, grasps his left elbow in his right hand and throws. (If, after ducking under *Uke*'s arm, *Shi* takes a step with his right foot and enters to *Uke*'s rear, he may attack the enemy's ribs with his right elbow and push him down [in *Kaiten Nage* fashion].)

86. *Uke*: Grasps *Aite*'s right wrist with his left hand.

Shi: Immediately upon being grabbed, advances [at an angle] on his right foot then steps behind *Uke* with his left foot extending his right hand. (If *Uke* should pull his left foot back [to keep his balance] step (again) with your left foot and [throw] pulling the enemy's left sleeve or step out big with your right foot to *Uke*'s left.)

87. *Uke*: Same as in No. 86.

Shi: Advances his left foot in front of the enemy, at the same time stretching his right arm across the front of his neck. Then stepping in behind *Uke*'s back with the right foot and controlling his right arm with his own left hand, *Shi* [can] push him directly down or [throw across his leading right leg] to [his own] rear.

(2)

(An alternative is to [begin] by changing the grip with the left hand and stepping in behind the enemy with your right foot and tie up his neck under your right armpit. [*Uke*'s chin should be up as in No. 46.])

(1)

88. *Uke*: Same as above.

Shi: First strikes *Men* with his left hand, then takes the enemy's left hand with that hand and at the same time pulls his left foot around to the rear. Then controlling *Uke*'s left elbow with his right hand, *Shi* [now] thrusts and pins [using both hands].

89. *Uke*: Uses the same attack but pulls.

Shi: Striking *Uke*'s face with his left, forcefully thrusts out his held, right hand [to his right side] and raises it while his right foot steps in [to the enemy's left side] and stands on *Uke*'s left foot. Then, pushing the *Koshi* (hip region) with his right hand *Shi* forces *Uke*'s neck down [and throw].

90. *Uke*: Holds *Aite*'s (i.e. *Shi*'s) right hand with his left.

Shi: Stepping across in front of the enemy with his rear (left) foot and raising his right hand up from the inside, thrusts it in behind *Uke*'s neck [over the left collar bone]. Now advancing his right foot to *Uke*'s rear and bringing his left hand around the front of the enemy's neck and grasping the back of his collar with the right hand, *Shi* must advance deeply with his left leg. [Picture No. 4]

(2)

(*Shi* may, having thrust his right hand [over the right collar bone] in front of the neck, use his left hand to grab the front of the *Obi* and then cut down with his right hand. [Picture No. 3.])

(3)

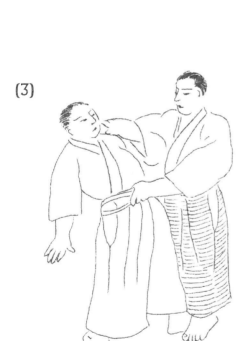

(4)

(1)

91. *Uke*: Same as above.

Shi: Takes one step forward with his right leg, swings his left foot around behind [himself and *Uke*], then throws the enemy to the rear. [Only the *Taisabaki* is shown in Picture No. 1 and 2.]

92. *Uke*: Same as before.

Shi: Thrusts out his held, right hand diagonally to [*Uke*'s] right front and taking hold of the enemy's left wrist with his own left, swings his left foot around to his rear. Then raising his right shoulder and pulling *Uke*'s left hand [causing an 'arm-bar'] *Shi* brings him down as his right leg advances behind the enemy's back.

(2)

(Or [after entering by the *Tenkan* movement of swinging the left leg around] *Shi* [can] punch the body with his right hand, dip his head deeply down while his right foot advances to the enemy's rear and his left hand extends out [and up] forcefully, then bring *Uke* over his back [leg] and throw big [to his own left].

Kokyu, (Ryote (Both Hands))

(1)

93. *Uke*: Grasps both of his *Aite*'s hands with both of his own, and puts out his right foot [assuming a *Migi-Hanmi* posture].

Shi: (1) If his stance is such that his leading foot is on the same side as *Uke*'s, in this case his left foot, [i.e. *Gyaku-Gamae*], *Shi* must put strength into his open hands and extend sufficiently while swinging his [trailing] right foot around to his own rear. [This movement is not illustrated.]

(2) On the other hand, should his right foot be forward, like *Uke*, [i.e. *Ai-Gamae*], *Shi* must advance boldly with his left foot [across, in front of *Uke*] and then turn [to throw].

(2)

Shiho Nage

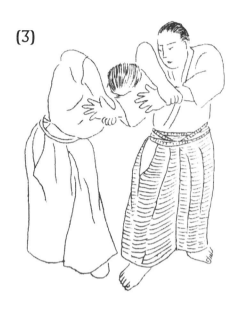

When the feet are the same as in the previous case numbered 'one' [i.e. *Gyaku-Gamae*], [*Shi*] grasps the opponent's right hand with his own right hand and raises them over his head [as he turns, thus producing *Shiho Nage*]. In a case such as Number 'two' [*Ai-Gamae*] advance taking the right hand in the right exactly as before [in case 'one'].

94. *Uke*: Grasps both of *Aite*'s hands with both of his own.

Shi: Advancing at an angle to his own left on his left foot then stepping in behind *Uke*'s right side with his right foot, extends his left hand [out], raises up his own right hand directly in front of himself, advances forward and cuts down across the enemy's neck.

95. *Uke*: Same as before.

Shi: Placing his right foot in front of the enemy, thrusts his right hand up toward the far side of *Uke*' neck with the feeling of pushing against it. Then he enters to the enemy's rear on his left leg [and extends his arms] palm facing up as [in the picture] at the upper left [P. 124].

(It is also possible to free your left hand and [use it to] grasp his left arm.)

[Note: Picture 'two' is drawn from the opposite side of Picture 'one'.]

96. *Uke*: Same as before [i.e. *Ryote Dori*].

Shi: Stands the fingers of both hands straight up at the instant of the attack while drawing his left foot back and, continuing back with the feeling of pulling, [ducks] his head throwing *Uke* over it to the rear.

(2)

(3)

(1)

97. *Uke*: Same as above.

Shi: Extends his right hand out at an angle to the enemy's right side while stepping in the same direction with his right foot.

(2)

(1)

98. *Uke*: Uses the same two-handed grip.

Shi: Begins advancing with his right foot, moving it in to the enemy's rear; then, raising his left hand in a pushing fashion up the front of *Uke*'s body and turning it toward his back on this side of his neck, cuts across the front of the neck toward the far side of the neck and pins. Should *Uke*'s left hand separate from *Shi*'s right, *Shi* should grab the back of the collar.

(2)

(1)

99. *Uke*: Same as above.

Shi: Raising his right hand around the outside, draws him up and in, then, taking one step forward with his right foot applies *Koshi Nage*.

(2)

(3)

(1)

100. *Uke*: Same as before.

Shi: [Sets up] *Koshi Nage*, [this time] by pulling his left leg.

(1)

101. *Uke*: Again, the same attack.

Shi: Advances on his right leg and strikes the face with his left hand. Stepping again, this time swinging the left foot back to the rear, [*Shi* must] lower his left hand sufficiently while raising his right hand.

(2)

(3)

(1)

102. *Uke*: Same as before.

Shi: Stepping in to his *Aite*'s left side with his right foot, thrusts his right hand to the enemy's right arm at an angle from the top of the elbow.

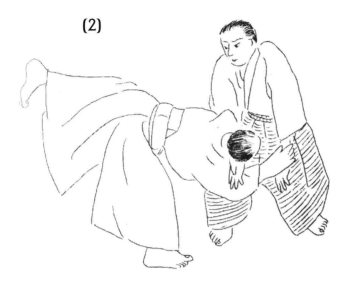

103. *Uke*: Applies the same two-handed attack.

Shi: Grasps the enemy's right wrist with his right hand, and thrusts his left hand out at an angle to his own right front, disengaging it. Then grabbing *Uke*'s left hand from above, *Shi* steps in with his left foot simultaneously turning under *Uke*'s arms and throws.

(2)

(3)

(1)

104. *Uke*: Same as before.

Shi: Crosses his right hand over onto the enemy' left from below, [thus] releasing his left hand to grab and pull the back of *Uke*' collar, or to [simply] punch to the face. [These two alternatives are not illustrated.] ([*Shi* may] extend his left hand across the front of *Uke*'s body, swing his right arm down under *Uke*'s legs and throw *with Sukui Nage* by moving in behind *Uke* on his leading, left leg [as in illustrations 'two' and 'three'].)

(2)

(3)

(1)

Mune (Chest; Collar, Neck)

105. *Uke*: Uses his left hand to grasp and pull *Shi*'s collar.

Shi: Strikes *Uke*'s face and takes hold of the hand at his neck with his right hand; then, dropping his *Koshi* slightly, steps in deeply with his left foot in such a way as to draw in [the attacker's right hand against *Shi*'s own body]. [*Shi* now] places his left hand onto the enemy's right elbow and pushes.

(2)

(1)

106. *Uke*: Grasps the chest as before but this time pushes.

Shi: While dropping back on his left leg and striking the face with his right hand, takes the enemy's right hand and moving his body in a stooped-over fashion, grabs the elbow joint with the left and pulls *Uke* down.

(2)

(3)

(1)

107. *Uke*: As above in 106.

Shi: Uses his left hand to strike the enemy's men and then to grasp his left hand. Drawing his left foot back, *Shi* wraps his right arm around *Uke*' waist and advances [in under] his front with his right foot. [*Koshi Nage* as in picture 'two']

(2)

([After the initial *Atemi* to the face, *Shi* may also] pull his left foot back, and take the enemy's left hand with his left while his right takes hold of the [elbow] joint; then regripping, with the left hand taking the back of the collar, uses his right to push the hips [from the rear forward]. When striking *Men* the right foot [should] come slightly to the right). [Not shown.]

(1)

108. *Uke*: As before, a one-handed grip on the front of the collar, [but this time with the right hand].

Shi: Inches his left foot outward and twists his body [to his right outside while striking to the face with his leading, left hand]; then stepping in with his right, advances to [his own] left front [i.e. *Uke*'s right side] and cuts down firmly on the left side of the enemy's neck.

109. *Uke*: Grabs as before [in 107] and strikes the face with his right hand.

Shi: Receives and cuts down the oncoming strike with his left hand, and passes it to his right hand. Then taking the hand holding his chest in his left hand, steps forward on the left foot and passes under [both the trapped arms].

(2)

(3)

(1)

110. *Uke*: Same as before.

Shi: Receiving [as before] with his left, strikes the face [by bringing his right hand around from the outside] and continues with [the right hand] entering [between the enemy's arms] from above [*Uke*'s left elbow], steps in on his right foot and ducks his head deeply [and throws] by pulling with his left hand. (Or, insert the right hand from above at the moment of the attack and without blocking the oncoming strike, dip the head and throw to the rear.)

(2)

(3)

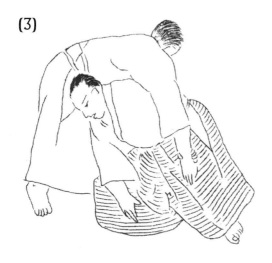

(1)

111. *Uke*: Again, grasps and attacks as before.

Shi: Swings his right hand around from the outside and stretches it directly across the front of the enemy's neck and advances on his right foot. ([Or] extend the right arm directly [from] where it is up the inside.)

112. *Uke*: Grabs deeply for *Shi*'s collar or chest with his right.

Shi: Strikes the face with his right [before *Uke* can get hold] then takes the extended right hand from below the wrist, and ducks around under that arm from the outside.

113. *Uke*: Holds the chest with his left and attacks with his right.

Shi: Receiving the strike with his right hand, takes one step [outside] with his left leg opening his body [to his own right]; then steps again with his right foot and cuts down onto the enemy's [left] shoulder.

(2)

(3)

(1)

114. *Uke*: Same as above.

Shi: Again receives with his right, then drawing his right foot back, uses his left hand to grasp and pull the enemy's left sleeve [from below].

(2)

115. *Uke*: Uses the same attack.

Shi: Pulls back on his right foot as in the previous technique and punches the body with his left hand.

(1)

(2)
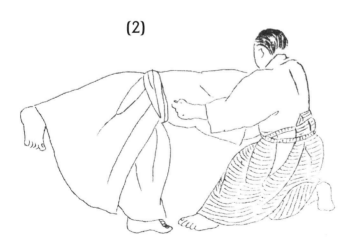

(1)

Mune to Te (Chest and Hand)

116. *Uke*: Takes hold of *Aite*'s [right] hand with his left and with his right, grasps the chest.

Shi: If pulled, should swing up his right hand in the direction it is being pulled as if raising [a sword] and advance on his left foot; then step in behind the enemy with his right foot and cut him down.

(2)

(1)

117. *Uke*: Same as above.

Shi: While swinging his right hand around from the outside and inviting the enemy in, takes hold of the right sleeve with his left hand and steps out on his left foot. Then entering with a step by the right foot, he [re]grabs the left sleeve with his left hand and pulls.

(2)

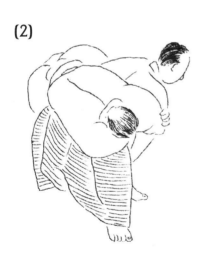

(1)

118. *Uke*: Same as before, [i.e. left hand on *Shi*'s right wrist and right hand at his chest].

Shi: Immediately upon being grasped on the right hand, thrusts it outward at an angle to his left front and steps in the same direction with his left foot. Then, regripping with his left hand *Shi* uses his right to grab the enemy's right sleeve [from below] and steps forward on his right leg.

(2)

(1)

119. *Uke*: Again takes the wrist and chest.

Shi: Moves in behind his opponent with his right foot and uses his left hand to regrasp the enemy's left wrist thus freeing the right hand, which may then take hold of the back of the collar while the left hand proceeds directly across and around the neck [from the front].

(2)

Kubijime (Strangle Hold)

120. *Uke*: Takes hold of the collars with the hands crossed over the other and chokes.

Shi: Grabs the enemy's left sleeve with his right hand and then stepping back sufficiently with his right foot, punches the body with his left hand.

(1)

121. *Uke*: Same attack. [*Kata* illustrations for No. 121 continue under pictures and text No. 122.]

[*Shi*: Applies *Atemi* to the enemy's face.]

(2)-a

122. *Shi*: **(1)** While punching the face with his right, inserts it from above, and inches back on his left foot; then turning around underneath from the enemy's left side extends both arms, just as they are, straight out.

(2) [Or] after passing under the arms, *Shi* may pull his right hand out and strike *Do* [as in Picture (2)-b].

(3) [Then again], having withdrawn the right hand, he may use it to take hold of the *Obi* and pull it up.

(2)-b

(2)-c

(1)

123. *Uke*: Same as the preceeding techniques.

Shi: Pushes up the enemy's hands with one shoulder then performs *Seoi Nage*.

(2)

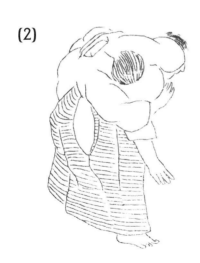

(1)

124. *Uke*: Same as before.

Shi: Inserts his hand from below between enemy's arms and onto the enemy's left sleeve, then advances forward on his left foot while pushing down *Aite*'s head with his right hand. ([Or,] drawing his left foot back while striking the face and then grabbing the enemy's right sleeve with his left hand, *Shi* enters from *Uke*'s right and pins *Uke*'s neck with his right hand.) [This technique does not appear in the illustrations.]

(2)

125. *Uke*: Again tries to strangle.

Shi: Putting his right hand in from below, extends it sharply [straight to the face], then stepping in with the right foot to the enemy's right side, brings his left hand up to suppress the head. [Picture 'two'] ([Other possibilities are] to grab the *Obi* with the right hand while advancing the left foot in behind the enemy, and use the left hand to push [back] the forehead; or, use the right hand from above [downward] and step in on the left foot.)

(1)

126. *Uke*: Same attack.

Shi: Extends his right hand boldly from below toward the enemy's right shoulder, then cuts downward while the right leg moves in to *Uke*'s left rear.

(2)

(1)

127. *Uke*: Same as before.

Shi: Puts out his right hand from below [and between *Uke*'s arms] and slides it around his neck from the left shoulder; then advancing [diagonally] to the enemy's left rear and bringing his left hand up behind the head, takes his own hand and locks the enemy's neck for the pin.

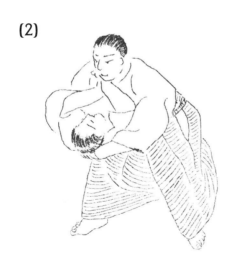

(2)

(1)

128. *Uke*: Applies the same choke.

Shi: Takes hold of his own clothing with his right hand, just below the point held [by the enemy], and uses his left hand to grab the lowest of the attacking arms from below and swings his left foot around to his rear, thus opening his body to the left. (Or, taking hold of his own collar with both hands in such a way as to open it [*Shi* may also] enter from the left.)

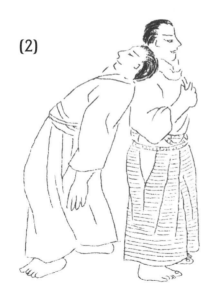

(2)

129. *Uke*: Same as above.

Shi: Thrusts out his right hand to the enemy's right side and advances his right foot to the enemy's right side [moving] toward his left rear, or conversely, may pull the left foot back with good effect. (Apply the right hand over the enemy's arms from above and extend both hands, then pull the left foot back and cut down.)

130. *Uke*: Same as before, [but from left *Hanmi*].

Shi: Slides his left foot in behind the enemy and brings his left arm up and over both the attacking arms and takes hold, then uses his right arm to scoop to *Uke*'s right leg.

(1)

131. *Uke*: Same [left-footed] attack.

Shi: Bends down and strikes the top of the enemy's leading foot (or, uses both hands to pin his right leg [as in No. 30].)

(2)

(1)

132. *Uke*: Same [*Kubijime* attack but from *Migi Hanmi*].

Shi: Drops his right hand in [between *Uke*'s arms] from above and spins in a big turn to his own left to wrap his left arm around the enemy's neck, trapping it in his armpit.

(2)

133. *Uke*: Same attack.

Shi: Swings his left hand up and at the same instant, brings his head around from the enemy's left side and inserts it between his arms. Then, stepping his left leg in behind, *Shi* extends his left arm and uses it to strike down and throw to the left rear [i.e. his and the enemy's].

Ushiro-Eri (Back of the Collar)

134. *Uke*: Holds the back of *Shi*'s collar with his right hand.

Shi: Simultaneously steps straight back on his right leg and swings up his right hand and attacks the enemy's face with [the back of] the left hand. Next, *Shi* draws his left foot deeply back, thus escaping to the rear of the attacking right arm, and grasping the wrist in his right hand and pushing down on the elbow with his left, steps out again on his left foot and throws big in a forward direction.

(3)

(4)

(1)

135. *Uke*: Same as No. 134.

Shi: Drops back slightly on his right foot and extends his left arm palm up and, keeping his own body straight, cuts directly down.

(2)

136. *Uke*: Same [*Migi-Hanmi*] attack.

Shi: [Again] inches back on his right foot [and tries] to strike *Men* with his left fist.

Uke: Blocks *Shi*'s attacking left with his own left and grabs the wrist.

Shi: Without breaking his left hand free, pulls his left foot back behind *Uke* and cuts straight down his left [as in No. 134].

137. *Uke*: Holds the rear of the collar with his right hand.

Shi: Strikes to the *Do* (trunk) with his left while turning to his own left (by drawing his left foot back [to his own rear]). Then stepping in again, this time on his right foot, *Shi* pushes the enemy's chin with his right hand.

138. *Uke*: Grabs the rear of the collar with his right hand and uses his left to hold *Aite*'s left wrist.

Shi: Pulls his right foot back and so faces half way to the right, then pulls his left leg and sticks out behind the enemy's back. Then, with his left arm coming from *Uke*'s front, *Shi* inserts his right between the enemy's legs [from the rear] and scoops them up.

139. *Uke*: Applies the same attack as in No. 138.

Shi: While pulling back his right leg deeply to the right rear and inducing *Uke* forward by [extending] the left hand, *Shi* simultaneously strikes the enemy's right armpit and overcomes him [by turning his body to face in the opposite direction].

(2)

(1)

140. *Uke*: Same as before.

Shi: [After the initial *Kamae* as shown in Picture 'One'] raises his left hand and bending his body to the left, ducks his head under [*Uke*'s left arm] and beats the enemy down to the right front.

While raising the left hand, instantly pull the right foot to your rear and strike his *Suigetsu*; then draw the left foot back and pull him down in front of you, [for one variation]. Then again, begin pulling the left foot back, then pull your right foot back behind the enemy and duck your head under his left arm and bring it down in front of you. Now grab the back of his collar with your right hand, and swing your left foot around from the front and, advancing to the enemy's rear, extend your left hand.

(2)

Or, pull the right foot to the rear, duck your head under his left arm thus turning [him] to your front. Put your right hand between his arms and extend it directly out. Once more, *Shi* may, in the same way drop back to the rear and twist his right arm around [*Uke*'s arms] from the top and throw to the front. [Or] wrap the right arm around the enemy's trunk and throw to the front [as in Picture 'two'].

(3)

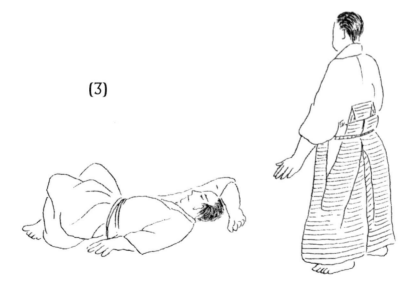

Kata (Shoulder)

141. *Uke*: Takes hold of both the enemy's shoulders with both of his hands.

Shi: Raises his left hand in suck a way as to surround [and protect] the head, and at the same time takes a half a step forward on his left foot, lowers his *Koshi*, and performs a *Kaiten* movement to the right. Then, as his feet advance in to the enemy's rear, *Shi* extends his left elbow or both arms sufficiently to throw to the enemy's left rear corner.

(3)

(4)

(1)

142. *Uke*: Takes hold as before and pulls.

Shi: As he is pulled, steps back lightly on his right foot and pulls his left back behind *Uke*, at the same time attacking his *Suigetsu* with the left elbow and defeats him.

(2)

(1)

143. *Uke*: Takes the same grip and pushes.

Shi: In the same manner as in technique 141, *Shi* spins to the right and at the same time grasps the enemy's right hand, puts strength into his left and pulls his left foot to the left rear using his left hand to strongly strike the enemy's left arm and overcome him.

(2)

(3)

(1)

144. *Uke*: Grabs as before and pushes.

Shi: Turning just as in No. 141, enters on his right foot, pushes the head down with his left hand and punches the body with his right.

145. *Uke*: Same hold but pulls.

Shi: Steps back with his left foot then pulls his right foot deeply to the rear bringing his head out behind the enemy's arm. Using his left hand to hold down the enemy's neck and his right to hold the *Obi*, *Shi* applies [*atemi*] with his chin to *Uke*'s side.

(1)

146. *Uke*: Same as above.

Shi: Turns only his left heel and pulls his body to the left, dropping his head down and bringing it out along with his own right arm behind the enemy's left arm, so that the right arm can be applied across *Uke*'s arms from above; then pushes with his *Koshi* to his right side.

(2)

(1)

147. *Uke*: Same as above [as in No. 146].

Shi: Pulls his left foot back to the enemy's right side, then takes hold of *Uke*'s legs with his left arm from above and his right arm from below and raises them up [for the throw].

(2)

(3)

(1)

148. *Uke*: Same as before.

Shi: Drops his left foot back to the enemy's rear, bringing his head out behind *Uke*'s right arm and takes hold of his head with both hands, right from the top and left from below, and twists.

(2)

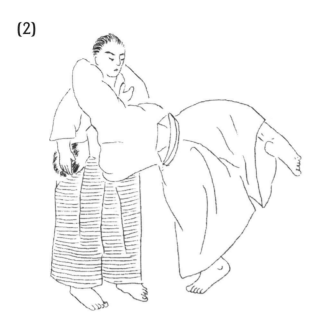

(1)

149. *Uke*: As before [takes hold of both shoulders from behind].

Shi: Raises his right hand and turns to [his own] left by swinging his right foot around from the front. [Then,] passing his [head and] right hand [over *Uke*'s left arm and out] under *Uke*'s [right] arm, *Shi* extends and cuts down [with that same, leading hand].

(2)

(1)

Ude (Arms)

150. *Uke*: Uses both hands to grip *Aite*'s two arms just below the elbows.

Shi: Pulls both elbows up and back at the instant of the attack, then bending down from the waist to the front, pulls his left foot back to his own left and [steps] in behind toward the enemy's left rear and throws him down face up.

(2)

(3)

151. *Uke*: Same as before but now pushes forward.

Shi: Raises his right hand up [to his forehead] and advances on his right foot; then, turning to the left, he pulls down *Uke*'s neck with his right hand and the left sleeve with his left.

(1)

152. *Uke*: Same as above.

Shi: Draws his right foot back behind *Uke*'s left side and follows with his body. Then taking *Uke*'s left arm with his own left and pinning it to his chest, *Shi* uses his right hand to push the enemy's left elbow and force him down to the front.

(2)

(3)

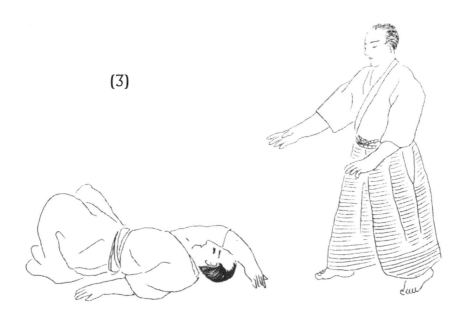

(1)

153. *Uke*: Uses the same [*Ushiro* attack].

Shi: Raises both arms and draws back slightly on his right foot, then steps again deeply around to his own [right] rear, and at the same time, strikes the enemy's face with his right hand and *Uke*'s [exposed] right side with the left.

(2)

(3)

(1)

Tekubi (Wrist)

154. *Uke*: Grasps both of *Aite*'s wrists with his hands from the rear.

Shi: Pulls back slightly on his right foot and [raising his right hand quickly] ducks under it by turning around to the [left] front. Then pulling his left foot back behind the enemy, and taking *Uke*'s left elbow in his left hand, uses his left foot again to advance forward, pushing and pinning.

(2)

(3)

(1)

155. *Uke*: Same as above.

Shi: Turns his right foot around the front to the left, at the same time raising his right hand; then continues turning once more to the left, extends both arms reversing *Uke* to a face up position and overcomes him in this manner.

(1)

156. *Uke*: Same as in the preceeding techniques.

Shi: Leads both the left hands to his own left front and turns his right hand toward *Uke*'s right side; then pulling to the rear on his own right foot, leans his body in that direction and strikes down to the right rear.

(2)

(3)

(1)

157. *Uke*: Same as above.

Shi: Simultaneously steps forward on his right foot and turns his palms up while thrusting both hands out and raising them to his head, then quickly [turns by] pulling his left foot back to the enemy's right side, cuts down to the front with both hands, duck his head and throws big in a forward direction.

(2)

(3)

(4)

(1)

158. *Uke*: Same as above.

Shi: Raises both his hands up without stepping forward then simultaneously drops his right foot back to the enemy's left side and lowers his arms to throw to the front.

(2)

(3)

201

(4)

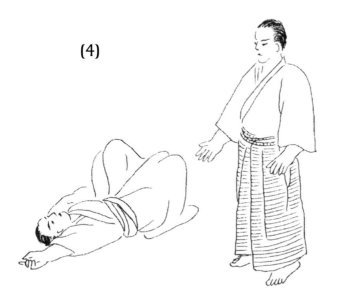

(1)

159. *Uke*: Same [*Ryote Dori*] attack.

Shi: Responds as in No. 158 except that he draws his right foot straight back between *Uke*'s legs, then pulls and throws.

160. *Uke*: Same as above.

Shi: Moves his body to the rear by drawing his right foot then pulling his left foot back to *Uke*'s right rear; now, using his right hand to pull to the right side, *Shi* cuts down with both arms and throws to his front.

(2)

(1)

161. *Uke*: Same as above.

Shi: Bends his right arm back, raises and ducks under his left arm, then applying his right shoulder enters to the inside of the enemy's left arm while bending his right hand forward wrapping it around [*Uke*'s] right elbow. Now with a step forward on his right foot (*Shi* throws) by pulling on the [enemy's] left arm.

(2)

(1)

162. *Uke*: Same as above.

Shi: Backs up on his left foot then drops deeply behind the enemy's left rear with his right foot. Next, using his left hand to grasp *Uke*'s right wrist, *Shi* frees his right hand to punch to the body.

(2)

(1)

163. *Uke*: Same as before.

Shi: Raises both hands and steps forward on his left foot. Then turning to the right with a *Kaiten* movement he advances to the enemy's rear on his right foot and extends his right arm firmly. (It is also effective to raise the left hand and pull the right hand.)

(2)

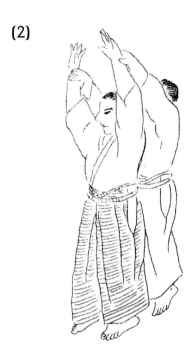

(3)

(1)

164. *Uke*: Same attack.

Shi: Raises both hands and escapes to the left rear, stands on *Uke*'s right foot and forces his neck down with his left hand.

(2)

(1)

165. *Uke*: Holds as before and pulls.

Shi: Bends his upper body deeply forward and stretches both hands up with palms facing up. Then extending the body and pulling his right foot to the enemy's left rear, *Shi* strikes *Uke* down to his own rear. [The throw is not shown in the pictures.]

(2)

166. *Uke*: Uses both hands to grasp and raise both of *Aite*'s wrists from below.

Shi: Drops his right foot back to *Uke*'s left rear; then sticking his left hand to his own *Koshi* and extending his right arm, uses it to cut down across the enemy's chest region.

(2)